MAMMAMITH

THE UNOFFICIAL MÅNESKIN BIOGRAPHY

www.dorakiki.com
London, U.K
Publisher ©2022 Dora & Kiki Ltd.
Author ©2022 Meltea Keller

DORA & KIKI

*Thanks to Eliselle,
without whom I would not have done
many things – including
writing this book.*

Introduction

Rock is dead! We've heard it so many times. The most notorious being in the early sixties when the genre was still classic rock and roll. Decca Records dismissed the Beatles because: "guitar groups are on the way out." Decca then hire the Rolling Stones, to reverse the epic mistake they had made.

The rest is history.

The point is: rock, like everything else, evolves through time. It has been pop-rock, acid, glam, prog, heavy metal, alternative and more... That's a lot of ways to present a musical setup made of guitars, keyboards, drums, bass, and voice in which instinct and rusty sound are distinctive elements. Not to mention the refusal of the geometric comfort zone of pop music (which it has a lot in common with anyway).

In pop and rock one thing happens (and I quote Carl Wilson in that essay called; '*Let's talk about love*' about Celine Dion, which in Italy they translated as "Shit music" – I'm not kidding!): every generation loves those who have characterized its history, its values and its (counter) culture. As for Måneskin, they are today's glam rock.

Those who have another idea of rock can say what they want: that the style of music isn't new, nor the sound, that they came from a talent show, that today's rock is a genre where musicians struggle in the underground and it won't make you become a star...

So what?

It's now been almost fifty years since the possibility that something could actually be new is questioned, now opting in favor of the idea that a creative genius recomposes what one has already seen or heard in an original way (this is key to Andy Warhol's poetics – and to the success of Lady Gaga). Today's talent shows are the breeding ground for a certain type of music – Eurovision is one of the ways to acquire international fame – facing them, or staying in the underground is the only choice.

What is certain is that Damiano, Victoria, Thomas, and Ethan are remarkable performers. They thrill, they're outrageous, they work hard and toy with people's fantasies... By putting themselves on stage, they embody part of a generation that, like them, is fluid and complex but, unlike some adults, lives consciously in the present. "*Sono fuori di testa*" they are out of their minds, but different from the ones before. That said with pride, revenge, and a shred of screamed suffering.

"Many countries," declared Victoria De Angelis live from Eurovision before the end of the competition, "did not expect a song like that [*Zitti e Buoni*] coming from Italy." There you go, it's time to say it: rock *does* exist in Italy. It's not well promoted; the majors don't believe in it, but it exists.

In the seventies, speaking of the progressive rock genre, PFM had a certain success abroad. As did other interesting bands; Area, le Orme, Banco di Mutuo Soccorso... Ivan Graziani was also an important guitarist and songwriter. Vasco Rossi, on the other hand, is for those who love less sophisticated sounds, while Litfiba went from rock to pop.

In the nineties, Marlene Kuntz left their mark. As for the underground, we had Diaframma, Massimo Volume, and Mumble Rumble; the first Italian all-female rock band. In alternative metal, Lacuna Coil is still rather important. A special mention goes to Afterhours and their front-man – Manuel Agnelli – who is often mentioned in this story and who has always believed in Måneskin.

So, if rock's dead, don't panic. It always comes back.

Or, to quote Damiano: "Rock and roll never dies!"

Table Of Contents

Part 1.

The origin and the get-together

If the entire superstructure is removed,
we are just four friends playing together
[Damiano]

Damiano

D amiano David was born in Rome on January 10, 1999, he's the only one in the band to have been born in the previous millennium. As an adult, he will describe his family as 'average' and in terms of economic availability, this is probably true. The little "not-so-average" detail is that both his Mom and Dad are flight attendants – this led little Damiano and his brother Jacopo (who later graduated in Agriculture), to travel around the world from an early age. The David-Scognamiglio family is a solid and supportive foundation, even cousins, of all different ages, helped Damiano in growing and comparing experiences. His mother, Rossella, went to school with the singer-songwriter Jovanotti, an important figure for Italian music, if not for anything else, then for having introduced the language of rap – mixed funky – into mainstream pop.

Damiano has several phobias, including vertigo and claustrophobia. As an adult, he will do parachuting, hoping that it would help him to overcome his fear of heights – but instead, his phobia will get worse.

His first memory linked to music is the song *Salirò* (*I will go up*), written and performed by the Roman-born singer-songwriter Daniele Silvestri, in 2002.

Regarding soccer, Damiano supports Rome. As a child, his father took him to the stadium and away matches. "Whether it was sunny or cold, we spent afternoons drinking Caffè Borghetti to warm up on away matches."

Damiano doesn't play any instruments – he just strums the guitar. However, singing is something that comes naturally to him from an early age. So much so that in primary school – while Vic did something similar with her friends – he wrote in an assignment: "I am Damiano and when I grow up, I want to be a *rockstar."* Later, he will tell the newspaper *Il Corriere della Sera:*

> "I remember that around the age of fourteen, when one starts to wake up a little, I used to watch pictures of various singers with their arms outstretched, in front of these massive audiences. They looked powerful, cool. I wondered: why them and not me? I'm healthy, I got everything I need, let's try. Singing made me feel good, I felt calmer. At first, you feel ashamed, you feel too many eyes on you, but at some point, you realize that those eyes on you are a good thing."

Before rock, however, Damiano used to play basketball. During the phase from childhood to his teenage years, he was a good, fast playmaker in the EuroBasket, Rome. He always recognized that he learned a lot from sport:

"I am a former basketball player and I often played in a big team, the discipline comes from there and, yes, I am the type of guy who sets rules, the ball-busting type. I am very strict with myself, and if I want others to do like me, I have to set a good example."

Massimiliano Ricca, his old coach, remembered Damiano as a basket player:

"He started at San Raffaele, a mini-basketball school on Portuense, in his neighborhood. Then, like all children, he began the rigmarole of EuroBasket, first as a beginner, then as an under thirteen, fourteen, and fifteen. He played until he was seventeen – that is the age when you decide to become a professional, semi-professional, or you quit. And he had other things to do, other talents to cultivate. He was a regular starter, an excellent player, and a smart guy; able to juggle in any situation, and to turn even unfavorable situations to his advantage. A smart-ass, as we say in Rome."

During his early teens, Damiano was a quiet, clean-cut boy. He already impressed the girls, who were often older than him. His 'first time' was at thirteen-fourteen, that's what he will confess to *Cosmopolitan* years later, adding: "But I have always hung around with older guys: my brother, my cousin... I always went out with them. Even in basketball, I was in a team of older kids".

When choosing a high school, Damiano decided on Liceo Linguistico Montale (a foreign language focused High

School), in the north of the Monteverde district. Yet, he didn't really fit in there. "For years I was told that I shouldn't think about music, I had to commit to something serious to be a responsible adult," he will say years later. Although from the recent interviews in English we notice a certain predisposition for languages – almost natural in those who learn to sing self-taught – Damiano actually flunked school twice.

Speaking of school, in the press conference after *X-Factor* he said:

> "Maybe I did it [X-Factor] also thinking a bit about my school history, which had never been brilliant. I have always considered myself a clever person, unfortunately a bit lazy in that area. Yet, I have often been told that in life I would not have achieved anything and to these people, I send my left buttock."

... The one with the '*Kiss This*' tattoo.

On the other hand, school today is a whirlwind of bureaucracy. There are countless talks going on about encouraging divergent intelligence but between saying and doing there's always a big gap. Damiano's former Principal, after the Sanremo Music Festival, released some statements full of esteem and compliments for the singer. Yet, in an interview with the newspaper *Il Fatto Quotidiano*, it turned out that during high school, the situation was tense between the two.

After X-Factor, Damiano flunked one more time and finally quit high school. He's the only member of Måneskin who hasn't finished his formal education. Speaking of which, he will tell the newspaper *Il Messaggero*:

"School? Yes, I do go back there to show them how cool I am. In theory, but very much in theory, I should have finished it. They rejected me twice, and after *X-Factor* came the third occasion. I didn't like school, being told what to do and not being able to express my intelligence. If you are not scholastically intelligent, it does not mean that you are not bright."

And again: "At a certain point, messing up in school was deliberate, it was very hard for me to sit and listen to someone telling me things for six hours. I wanted to jump on the judges' table and break everything" – like he did on his first X-Factor live show.

Yet, a professor from Liceo Montale – not one of Damiano's, but one in charge of organizing the high school choir – shared his memories after Eurovision:

"I remember one of his first performances, he sang *Your Song* by Elton John and I immediately realized he had great charisma, everyone in the audience was enraptured. He had this gift of captivating listeners, even though I met students at school with a better vocal tone than his. He was a nice guy, very humble, I never expected that from the choir of Montale he would get so far."

At sixteen, something happened; a change that led Damiano to leave basketball for music. He finally began to take singing seriously. As he told *Vanity Fair*:

"I used to be a wholly different person. I was very introverted; I was always on my own. Physically I was also different: short hair, no tattoos, no earrings, laced shirt. I lived to be accepted, to please others. Then I realized that I had to answer only to myself. I met them, Måneskin were born, and they gave me a great personal upgrade. I realized that I could express myself and when you do, others appreciate you more because they see you as you are."

Talking to *Il Messaggero*, he added:

"A lifetime ago, I was a different person: I wore my hair short and neat, I played basketball, I didn't sing. Then, the revolution, thanks to a group of crazy friends, who encouraged me to be as I like: at first, I hid myself to avoid unwanted remarks that made me anxious. At a certain point, I understood that it was the people who yelled at me that had to hide."

The group of crazy friends was composed of Thomas, Ethan, and Vic.
A journalist at Eurovision asked what kind of unwanted remarks bothered Damiano: "Comments on our sexuality or, like, you're a man you don't have to wear make-up, and all this stuff. At the beginning it's tough, but with time you get used to that, and it goes away."
Fun Facts: when Damiano finds a bed with blankets tucked under the mattress, he either pulls them all out or he can't sleep. His favorite series is the anime *Death Note*. He got his first tattoo the day after he reached the age of majority, as he hadn't previously had parental permission. His first crush, as a good former basketball player, was on Lola Bunny.

Vic

Ethan Torchio once said:
"Vic is one of the nicest people in the world, she makes hilarious jokes. Besides, she is a problem solver, she has a super-smart mind."

Victoria De Angelis was born in Rome on April 28, 2000. Jeanett Uhrbrand, her mother, was Danish. She and Alessandro (aka Sandro), Victoria's father, founded De Angelis Viaggi, a tour operator agency with Italian-Scandinavian staff to guarantee a prompt response to the needs of Nordic tourists; it is the family business. The tour operator is a profession somewhat similar to that of Damiano's parents, certainly both figures have to do with international openness.

In October 2003, Veronica (aka Nica), younger sister of the future bassist, was born. She has a darker, less Scandinavian skin tone.

Fun Facts: since she was little, Vic has emetophobia (a phobia of vomit). In kindergarten, when a classmate threw up, a teacher told her: "Don't look. Otherwise, you'll vomit too," and this kind of shocked her. Although, it's not true what they reported in an interview: "when Vic sees her fans, she turns her back to them for fear that they might vomit". That would be a little awkward, right? Her first crush was on Edmund, from *The Chronicles of Narnia*.

As a child, Vic was a blonde girl with big eyes. Certainly, not the pink princess type. Later, she will declare to *Il Corriere della Sera*:

"I didn't really go through that phase... I had no female friends, I was not interested in combing my hair, playing with dolls... I find it absurd that already at 6-7 years old one can be shaped by the conventions of society. Something is changing, certain ideas need to be dismantled, but the path is still long. If you use strong language, they say: 'you are not talking like a young lady.'"

As she grew up, she fitted less and less into the cultural definition of what a girl should or shouldn't be. As she told the magazine *Elle*:

"A certain rigid distinction between masculine and feminine made me suffer: at the age of six, I refused all girly things: I skated, I kept my hair short, I dressed like a boy. I didn't wear skirts, not because I didn't like them, but to reclaim the chance to be myself. Rock embodied that momentum of freedom."

Around the age of eight, she began to get passionate about music. "I started with the guitar," she said to *Il Corriere della Sera:* "self-taught, after having seen a not-so-famous Danish film in which there was a child who played it." Her first lesson is still on YouTube: Vic, very blond and profoundly serious, sits on an unmade double bed with a Fender-like guitar bigger than her in her hands. She plays a classic for beginners: the riff of Deep Purple's *Smoke on the water*. For a first-timer, she's not bad at all. Some cute pictures that Vic uploaded on Instagram must be more or less from that period: she and another child with a guitar, strike rock star poses while on a piece of paper they wrote '*rokc* studio'

Years later, the bassist will tell her high school's online newspaper:

"So, I started playing the guitar when I was about 8 years old, I played it with a friend of my Mom's in a very informal way, I didn't take real lessons. Then at the "*scuole medie*", I chose those with musical direction where I actually had guitar as a subject – there I started studying classical guitar in a little more in-depth way. At the "year-end performance" of the *seconda media* [seventh grade], the teacher made me play the bass and from that moment on I started with that. Then I had all my various small bands and I got more and more passionate, but I didn't take lessons anymore."

'Scuole medie' is middle school in Italy: three years from about eleven to fourteen years old. When middle school has no particular direction, during music lessons, everyone plays the recorder; an instrument considered egalitarian because it's more or less easy for everyone (although they do give a small keyboard to those with posture or breathing problems). Middle schools with musical direction, on the other hand, offer the possibility of learning a more useful instrument: guitar, piano, violin, flute, etc. Vic – and soon we'll see, Thomas too – at the age of eleven chose this type of institution. "From there, I started playing bass," she will admit during *X-Factor:* "because I sucked too much at playing the guitar."

As for the rest, life for the future Måneskin bassist resembles that of many teenagers: school, friends, happiness for the snow of 2012 (it seldom happens in Rome), skateboarding, rock... At the age of twelve, in the areas around the Quattro Venti railway station or at Chiesa Nuova, Vic became passionate about skateboarding. She learned the spins, the ollie, and the cursed kickflip, for which she asked for advice on Facebook... She used to spend time trying tricks with the board listening to Pantera, Eminem, Gemitaiz, Led Zeppelin, Guns N' Roses, Nirvana (her first CD was *Nevermind*) and Green Day. She also used to discuss animatedly, as a young music lover with already very well-defined tastes, with friends about songs to put under the skating videos. In brief, Vic was a skater. She even participated in skating contests and was a regular customer of a street sports shop in Monteverde called Slug. Among her favorite music was: Metallica, Bring me the Horizon, Arctic Monkeys, Sex Pistols, Joy Division, Blondie, Marylin Manson, Die Antwoord, AC/DC, David Bowie, The Rolling Stones, and Sonic Youth. Years later, Vic will talk about how Kim Gordon influenced her:

> "The one who inspired my imagination is Kim Gordon from Sonic Youth: in those years rock was a male world, she never cared about that, she messed up every stereotype of beauty, in her way of being on stage there is a certain amount of aggressiveness, she is also a bit coarse, thousands of people liked her because of her music."

Kim Gordon was born on April 28th, like Vic.
While her sister Nica became passionate about street dance, Vic started playing in small teenage bands around the age of fourteen. *Solipsism* was the first and it was exactly what you'd imagine a band of five fourteen-year-olds to be: some were serious, while others were less devoted to the music. Vic already stood out because of her long blond hair and her determination. Some videos are still online: Vic seems to believe in herself as a musician, even if now and then she stumbles into some bass lines – as you can hear from her first

gig playing *Personal Jesus*. Her Mom Jeanett really liked Depeche Mode.

In that period, Vic also got more and more into dressing with a rock style: from skater pants to fishnet tank tops, ripped pants, buffalo shoes and their huge wedges, miniskirts, neck studs, and a tongue piercing after the *terza media* (equivalent to eighth grade) exam.

Fashion still attracts her. During X-Factor, she said:

> "Whether it can be seen as a beautiful thing or a bad thing, objectively the first impression of you some might have comes from the visual impact, in the sense that when you see someone and you do not yet know him/her/them internally or emotionally, the first and only thing you can rely on, let's say, is aesthetics. This is crucial in a context like music where you have to impress the ones who see you because there are so many talented singers and artists, of course, and the difficult thing is precisely to stand out in my opinion, to be different from the crowd so that people remember you."

When the time came to choose a high school, Vic turned to the Liceo Classico Virgilio in Monteverde, it's a type of school that's focused on classic literature and languages like ancient Greek and Latin. Amongst the music she liked, there were Liszt, Beethoven, and King Crimson. Her new band was called 3rd Room, because they always rehearsed in classroom 3. The singer was a certain Damiano. Thomas Raggi, on the other hand, had met Vic around 2013, before Damiano, earlier in middle school.

They both had experience in various bands before. The guitarist recalls the moment he decided to call Vic and start a new band as follows: "In seventh grade I really liked the idea of playing with others, so I went to Victoria, we were at school together, and she said come with us, the singer is cool!" The 3rd Room didn't get very far. They wanted to play metal, while Damiano was looking for something more poppy. So, they kicked him out for artistic differences.

Instead, Thomas and Vic had remarkably similar tastes in music: Ramones, AC/DC, Guns N' Roses, Metallica... So, they started looking for a new singer and a drummer.

They did find a girl who was a good singer, but she came from outside Rome and it was hard for her to find time for rehearsals. Meanwhile, Damiano called Vic one more time swearing that he: "no longer sucked at singing" and had improved. Thomas and Vic gave him another chance, and took him back. That was November 2015.

After X-Factor, the front-man will describe the reference genres of each member of Måneskin as follows:

> "We come from four completely different backgrounds: she [Vic] is pop, he [Thomas] is rock and roll, he [Ethan] started out playing jazz and instrumental music while I started out as a soul singer, so the mixture of these things created Måneskin."

Måneskin were at the time four teenagers searching for their unique sound and exploring the music around them. That explains why Vic was deep into rock culture, yet also a fan of all those aspects related to fashion and appearance that belongs to pop.

It is around the end of 2015 that Jeanett falls ill with cancer. It's a story that Elin Uhrbrand, Vic and Nica's grandmother, told the magazine *Di Più:*

"My granddaughter Victoria suffered a lot; she saw her mother die. When my daughter, Jeanett, realized that she was going to lose the battle against the evil that was consuming her, she asked to go to Denmark. Victoria wanted to follow her and stayed close to her until the end... She was only fifteen years old. For three months she watched over her mother, for three months she held her hand. Until her dying day. Until she said goodbye. It was terrible."

Victoria left for Denmark with her mother in late fall – around the time David Bowie released the single *Blackstar*.
The fan base of The Thin White Duke could never have imagined what would happen in January. Jeanett and Bowie passed away a few weeks apart.
In interviews, Vic states that she started suffering from panic attacks at fourteen years old – so a year before her mother passed away. She tells *Elle*:

"I was a light-hearted girl, at fourteen I found myself not wanting to leave the house, I lost a year of school. Something was broken inside me and I didn't know how to fix myself. I used to be ashamed of this, now I don't need to hide it anymore."

It was a 'sinkhole' (her words) that Vic managed to tackle thanks to her family, therapy, music and the affection of friends.

Ethan

I generally speak if I have something to say
[Ethan to *Il Fatto Quotidiano*]

Damiano David once said:

> "Ethan is the guru of the 'philosophy of keep-fuckin-calm.'
> The world goes this way? He is above it. He looks at things
> objectively, the passionate side of things doesn't bother
> him, like a wise old Native American. He helps you; he
> always gives you another perspective."

Ethan Torchio (pronounced Torkio) was born on October 8,
2000, under the sign of Libra. He is the penultimate of
Måneskin to be born, but the last to be initiated into the band
– which is what happened decades earlier with Ringo Starr.
His Mom really liked Ethan Hawke: hence the unusual name
(in Italy). His father, Candido Torchio, is a director and DOP:
he worked as the director of photography on the video for *A
forma di fulmine* (*Thunder shaped*), a song by the singer-
songwriter Vasco Brondi.
"Ethan is never upset," said Vic during a live Instagram
broadcast before the first live show in Sanremo, the same
Instagram broadcast in which they reveal his hotel alias by
calling him Edgar (hotel alias are the names given in hotels
for celebrity reservations so that they can keep a low profile
– they are supposed to be secret). The typical cold-blood of
the drummer with long black hair, passionate in labyrinths
(of which he has drawn since he was ten), possibly comes
from his large family: "I have... Wait for me to stop and

count," he told *Cosmopolitan:* "six sisters (the eldest is forty-one, I think), two brothers, and one on the way. We have three different mothers." Among his sisters are the photographer Lucrezia and her twin sister Eleonora, an editing secretary and sound engineer, both working with their father. Not all the Torchio siblings look like Native Americans.

It's probably because of this background, linked to the family trade, that the others consider Ethan as the "nerd" of the group; the one who also knows a little about producing. Speaking of what Ethan learned from his large family, he said:

> "When the siblings are many, you are no longer just brothers or sisters. The type of relationship you have is more like friendship, I know it sounds bad but instead, it's beautiful. You are part of a community. This teaches you altruism, it makes you understand that if there is a problem, you have to solve it together. You put your efforts, everyone does their part, and you understand what to do, without leaving anyone behind."

Speaking about how he started to play drums, he told *Cosmopolitan:*

> "Since I was little, they tell me, I have been tapping on everything: with the cutlery, on the plates, on the furniture, on the wall. So, at five they gave me drums as a present. It had been in a box for a while, then I found it again while moving house. I pulled it out. It was not usual to have such a beautiful instrument, I wanted to take advantage of it and I started playing for real. I kept it in my father's house, in the countryside, in the province of

Frosinone. It was in my room: when I had to play, I took a mattress and put it in front of the door, so it muffled the noise. It fit perfectly."

Ethan spoke about his first 'gig' to the newspaper *Il Corriere della Sera:* "I played the theme of *Deep Red*, by Goblins. It had taken me two and a half months to learn it and I also played it badly. It was thrilling and traumatizing."

At the time, he was twelve.

On YouTube, there are also some videos of young Ethan studying: in the first one, the fourteen-year-old drummer practices very seriously on Nirvana's *In Bloom*. There is also a year-end performance organized by the Sonora Music Center in Castelliri, near Frosinone. That's the music school, in the village of Monte San Giovanni Campano, where Ethan studied music. In the video, the band plays *That's what you get* by Paramore and he, whom already had super long hair, is filmed the whole time from behind his back.

His teacher, Azeglio Izzizzari, spoke of him after the Sanremo Music Festival 2021:

"On Tuesday night I was watching the festival and, just before the Måneskin performance, my cell phone rang. On the other end was Ethan, who wanted to talk to me to thank me. I think I have just done a good job on a natural gift. Because he really is talented, though he and the other guys in the band spend hours and hours studying."

Basically, Ethan lived in Rome during the week, where he attended Liceo Artistico (Art School). Over the weekend he would then travel to his father's house in the small village of Colli, in the Frosinone area, where he parked his drums. The village had, at that time, about two hundred inhabitants, most of whom were Torchios.

His teacher's words, again:

"He has always been a well-mannered boy like all his siblings and his father, who decided to support him step by step. What I can say for sure is that he is still the smart, witty, and humble guy I met years ago. He just improved with me his natural gift. Playing well as he does is not for everyone, and it is not enough. One has to train and study. Ethan and the other members of the band understood this and that's how they managed to become such a smash. Sunday morning, I received a very long message from him in which he told me what it feels like to win the Sanremo festival and then he thanked me once again."

Fun fact: His favorite books are *Siddhartha* by Herman Hesse and *The Alchemist* by Paulo Cohelo, and from this, we can easily guess that Ethan is the band member most interested in spirituality. He has the habit of counting to ten before turning off the light and going to sleep. Some journalists have asked him if, when he thinks, he thinks with the "*r moscia*", which is typical of Ethan – this is when speaking in Italian, you are unable to roll your 'r' properly. Ethan's first crush, after a video he saw in Costa Rica, was at the age of seven – on Laura Pausini.

Thomas

Damiano David described him as follows:
"Thomas has a child's imagination. He is the youngest, and he is super-creative. He's the kind of guy that, if you give him a guitar, after five days you will still find him in the same position, still playing."

Thomas Raggi (pronounced Radji) was born on January 18, 2001.
He's a Lazio soccer team supporter. Lazio is also based in Rome, and is their biggest rival.
Like Victoria, he started playing as a child: at nine, after seeing some good guitarists, he asked for a guitar and got one from his father – who also works in the music business. His father was overjoyed, being himself a fan of Metallica and Led Zeppelin. The guitar is almost an obsession for Thomas, it's a monomaniac love, typical of those who do not choose – but are chosen instead – by music.
Years later he will define himself, plain and simple, as a "guitar maniac."

> "I knew it! I knew it was going to end like this: when I grew up, I wanted to make music, to play, to live the life of a band. And I said to myself: "In one way or another, I sure can do it." My only interest has always been music and music only. I gave up on doing many things to play."

The first photo that appears today by scrolling back on his old personal Facebook page is – guess what – a guitar. The date is October 8, 2013, and the caption reads: 'My Fender.' At twelve, Thomas was already playing in small school bands.

Slash is a name that already appears in posts from February 2014: Thomas shares the picture of the guitarist's Les Paul. The other hero he will remember in future interviews is John Frusciante, Thomas admires his ability to put a few notes in his solos – the right ones, at the service of the song. Another figure of inspiration for the young musician is Jimmy Page, of course. He inspired many.

In July 2014, Thomas is a thirteen-year-old blond teenager who looks even younger than his age. He was already nicknamed *Er Cobbra*, which is how they pronounce "the cobra" in the Roman dialect. While Vic, from her Facebook page, writes about how much she likes *Stairway to Heaven* and posted (among others) Metallica songs, Thomas – with his faithful yellow Fender in hand – filmed himself playing the introduction of Led Zeppelin's masterpiece and *Nothing Else Matters*. The first concert he ever attended was by Metallica. He and Vic knew each other since middle school and their friendship on Facebook is dated back to October 2013: later she chose Liceo Classico, a year later he will choose Liceo Scientifico (a school focused on sciences), also in Monteverde. Despite the different institutes, they still shared the desire to play in a band, which had pushed them both towards the musical direction in middle school.

Years later, Thomas will tell *Cosmopolitan* that Victoria has been the one who led him to understand and appreciate fashion: "It was she who first made me think about my look and these things, I didn't care about that stuff before. She is our advisor, in this sense." It was his way to express himself that, over time, the guitarist took seriously enough to earn the nickname, together with the bass player, 'cute little siblings.'

Fun fact: Thomas's favorite TV series is *Narcos*.

Måneskin?

The history of Måneskin begins in Monteverde, a central district of Rome in the Trastevere area near Porta Portese. Three out of four Måneskins were based there.

One of the first videos made by the three original members of Måneskin is dated November 2015 and it features only Damiano and Victoria playing Alt J's *Breezeblocks*. Below, on Vic's Facebook profile, Thomas Raggi writes: 'Guys you cut me out :D' Ethan would have joined the band shortly after that. Those were the days of the terrorist attack on the Bataclan concert hall in Paris, the days when Vic had to leave for Denmark for her last trip with her mother...

The bass player will explain the dynamics of the band's line-up to her school newspaper a year later, in January 2017:

> "We formed the band in November 2015, so we have been playing together for just over a year. I already knew and had played with the singer Damiano a few years before, he then contacted me with the aim of forming a group. We called Thomas (the guitarist) whom I knew because he was also in middle school with me and we found our drummer Ethan on a Facebook group for musicians."

In January 2018, Thomas will add that:

> "The first clear memory I have with the whole band is in the rehearsal room: after breaking the ice we immediately started to work, we didn't talk much, we just needed an 'and one, two, three' to start. You can picture the rest."

Facebook sometimes still provides good services; Ethan placed an ad: 'drummer looking for a group.' On the same group called 'Looking for musicians in Rome' Vic wrote: "We are looking for a drummer for a new wave band". Yes, she wrote "new wave", later she will confess that she labeled their music kind of randomly. Anyway, no one answered her, so she contacted Ethan, her only option. Thomas, Vic, and Damiano didn't have much to choose from. But, as they say, first choice, best choice.

In January 2018, the drummer will remember the first rehearsal as follows:

> "The chemistry between us was there from the first note we played together, the same chemistry that keeps binding us to this day, which inspires us creativity and in our search for unheard melodies. We were four ordinary guys, undemanding and without expectations, fueled with a lot of passion and team spirit; we were four guys unaware that we were watering a seed, which would become an imposing bush. There is still a long way to go, and we are ready to keep growing."

Damiano on the other hand, later confessed that sometimes during their first rehearsals, he was caught by laziness: "It was something I did just for fun, like we try once, twice a week, but sometimes I didn't feel like it, sometimes I pretend I had a fever. Nowadays it's different; rehearsing is an obsession to me."

Ethan, during that time, in addition to his familiarity with his instrument, surprised the others by being into aliens. However, Vic will then tell the radio personality JoJo Wright: the final choice that allowed the singer and drummer to stay in the band together was basically grounded by the experiences she and Thomas had with previous band

members: "They were very, very terrible", admits the bassist, "I still have videos on YouTube."
On the genre, not quite rock at the very beginning, Vic said after X-Factor that:

"When we started playing, we were fifteen, sixteen... we were really young so even as for personal identity we didn't have a clear idea of our style and in terms of music it was a bit like... it was a bit more for fun, like... the way we managed the project... So, we weren't really focused on what we wanted to do. Then after we took a trip to Denmark where we played three or four days together and we stuck together all the time, we understood that this was what we really wanted to do. From that moment on, everyone focused on their identity and therefore consequently also on the identity of the band."

Denmark, we will get to that.
The first Måneskin gig, as a quartet, was at the Sedicidiciotto restaurant on March 19, 2016. It was lightly that the *Pulse* festival – which we will mention later – was already in sight. The guys put up an exceptionally long set of thirty songs. "It was crazy!" Damiano said years later, "our set lasted two hours and forty minutes – all covers."
It must have been around this time that, when signing up for the *Pulse* competition, the group realized they didn't have a name: the boys then asked Vic to say some "random cool name" in Danish. One of the biggest puzzles a brand-new band faces was a done deal in about an hour. One of the words Vic said without thinking was *måneskin*, which means moonlight. "Let's keep it," the boys said, "we will change it in the future." Many years later, Damiano will comment on this

episode: "Then we never changed it because we are lazy asses."

What's certain is that Måneskin weren't lazy when it came to writing original songs: Damiano remembers how the first composing experiments started two weeks after the first time they played together – the four of them. "We felt something was going on, actually," he told Zach Sang the radio DJ: "It was not just a band to spend your afternoons with, it was something serious – so we said from the very beginning: let's write our own songs." It was a feeling, a deep feeling. It was realizing that everyone was giving their best: "We didn't have to talk about it," says Damiano, "it was natural." In her school newspaper during January 2017, Vic declared: "My dream would be to live off this profession and we are trying hard to make it happen together." From the very start, Måneskin sounds like a beautiful story where team spirit and friendship are a point of strength – and in an atomized world like ours, there is so much need for stories like that.

Victoria then began to influence Damiano in wearing makeup. As the singer recalls: "She was like, I think a little eyeliner looks good on you. I said, uh? Then I saw myself: how cool is that!?"

From the same period is a video in which Vic, Thomas, and Damiano play and sing an acoustic version of Stevie Wonder's *Master Blaster*. On Facebook, a friend of Vic's writes about Damiano: "Your voice is very good, why don't you go to *Amici* or *X-Factor*." (*Amici* is another historic Italian talent show on the Mediaset networks.)

Part 2.

Being a street busker group in Rome

Pulse

B efore their debut on the street as buskers – a forced choice not only for them but for anyone who wants to live off rock/pop music in Italy, today more than ever – Måneskin's real debut was at the *Pulse* contest.

Stepping back: what was it like to have a band in Italy pre-covid?

The situation of live music venues began to deteriorate in the early 2000s. The excessive costs that a small-medium venue has to bear, the increasingly pressing obsession with silence to be preserved in town centers (whoever knows the meaning of the term 'gentrification' knows what I'm talking about), the moving of rock clubs to the suburbs and the general flourishing of small places that don't pay much and are only suitable for songwriters or line-ups of one-two members has made (and probably will continue to make) the life of aspiring rock musicians very difficult.

After all, the Italian mainstream ceased to be interested in rock since about 2001. They don't want rock musicians; the radio stations seldom play rock music. It's easy to give up, also considering the uncertainty about whether a gig will be rewarded, given that sometimes (quite often), if they go overdrawn, the managers of the venues do not guarantee the agreed money.

So (pre-covid) in order to play, earn money, be heard, and be part of a network, an emergent band had two options: contests (the regular way) and busking (the tricky-but-rewarding way). This is why Måneskin chose to pick up a spot in via del Corso, a large street in the historical center of Rome, and perform as buskers, while they made their debut at the *Pulse* contest.

Pulse was an idea of the entrepreneur Matteo Caffarelli, in 2016 it took place in Rome (the venue was Wishlist in the quarter of San Lorenzo), and in Bologna (the venue was Arteria). It lasted for four editions, and it aimed to offer a space where teen bands could make their first gig, that's why the whole name of the event was 'Pulse High School Band Contest.' The previous name of the same show was *Maxsi Factor*, almost a premonition for Måneskin. There were twenty-four competing bands for each edition, then there was a 'technical jury' of experts – says Caffarelli, interviewed by Riccardo De Stefano, who in that period, directed the magazine *ExitWell*.

Pulse was an opportunity in short, and a tempting one, even for those who had never left the rehearsal room and for those who had never walked on a stage. The venues could take about 100/150 people, record company talent scouts and journalists often attended the gigs or were part of the jury.

In 2016, says De Stefano, Måneskin were vastly different from today. "The guys were between sixteen and seventeen years old, Damiano was the eldest, they had practically no experience." At the time, Matteo Caffarelli promoted the contest by reaching out to a number of high schools, spreading the word about *Pulse's* existence. That year, he also reached out to Ethan's school, Liceo Artistico. The drummer immediately realized that the opportunity was not to be let go and signed the band up.

After a few days, Caffarelli received a phone call: it was Ethan again. He expressed his second thoughts: the band wasn't ready, they had never played together except in the rehearsal room, they didn't even have a Facebook page... And the risk of messing up was just around the corner. Caffarelli, however, who must have already seen so many troubled rookies, made the drummer think. Ethan calmed down and the band remained in the contest. The drummer certainly could never have imagined that, with that same line-up, five years later they would open for the Rolling Stones.

But other test beds would come.

The patron of *Pulse* remembers the young Ethan Torchio like this: "Very shy, very private but also very profound, I remember him as a deep person." He describes Victoria as: "a typical teenager: bubbly and joyful, light-hearted and even a little frivolous, in the good sense of the term." Lightness was probably what Vic needed, a few months after those painful three months in Denmark. She was certainly, of the three instrumentalists, the one who cared the most about the look, with her fake Panama hat and psychedelic pop shirt against the creased T-shirts and jeans of her fellow musicians on the first night of Pulse. Caffarelli again says, this time about Thomas Raggi: "He didn't show much personality." Well, he was *the quiet one.* It must be a guitarist thing, a certain obsessive focus on the instrument that makes them look like silent types. Or simply, like George Harrison before him, Thomas was the youngest, the shyest. He was only fifteen. And besides, come to think of it, maybe in this story, the real *quiet one* is actually Ethan. Finally, Caffarelli describes Damiano David as: "A force of nature. A beautiful boy, a nice fellow too. I think he had never studied music, but he had this innate talent in singing and above all, in being on stage. He was cool, the way he moved... For being seventeen... He looked as if he was twenty."

Pulse began. Måneskin performed and made a splash. The quarter-finals, semifinals, and finals passed – they won the contest at the Wishlist on September 17, 2016. Not bad for a band that 'wasn't ready.' The first prize was an electric guitar, a three-gig tour, a studio recording, and a gig in the largest meeting event between labels, musicians, and professionals of the independent market in Italy: the MEI (literally the "meeting of independent labels") which takes place every year in the town of Faenza, in central-northern Italy. There are some very nice photos of Ethan on the train to Faenza reading a book on spirituality entitled *La bilancia cosmica (The cosmic balance)* with Damiano sitting by him, pulling faces at the camera. Another cute picture shows the four Måneskin members around the main square of Faenza with backpacks and guitars like they were on a school trip: it was their first concert outside Rome. About that period, Thomas Raggi will tell Zach Sang: "It was really important, especially on first gigs, when the people in front of us – like one person, two people in front of us – said 'oh wow, this band is cool, these guys are cool ' ...It was really motivating."

Fabrizio Galassi, journalist and former director of the magazine *Rockstar,* was in the audience during the *Pulse* semifinal. He was extremely impressed by Måneskin. "I had a feeling," he told Riccardo De Stefano:

"Of having witnessed something bizarre, starting from the chemistry of the room. The contest had these bands... that were really high school bands, with the audience basically made up of classmates, some friends and sometimes, some relatives. During a change of stage – we had the audience behind us – I felt a sensation, like a wave... like when a place fills up with people and you feel the wave of the heat coming. So, I turned around and saw the room full of kids, mostly girls. Suddenly, the whole school was in that room – and those from other schools too. When they came out and I saw the audience explode, especially for Damiano, considering the previous wave-like feeling, I told myself 'I want to see who the fuck these guys are' and when they left the stage they had already won, period. Damiano alone held the stage as if he were a thirty-year-old, forty-year-old. His English was good, his voice was super recognizable, the performance was good and he was in tune. Plus, he was really cool, even then."

Damiano showed up onstage with jeans, a creased shirt, Wolverine sideburns, no makeup, and no visible tattoos. It was he who initially caught everyone's attention – hiding, according to De Stefano, some coordination issues that made Måneskin, compared to some of the other bands, less precise music-wise. Davide Dose was also on the jury. He was the artistic director of the formula of musical evenings called Spaghetti Unplugged. That night Damiano impressed him so much that he felt the need to tell him: "Put less energy into what you do, you risk to overshine the others too much... Remember, you have a band." Dose himself recalls that many hyper-technical bands went to the final live show, yet the artistic project they had in mind was not so clear. Måneskin were the opposite of that, that's why they won over everyone.

"We didn't all share the same opinion in the jury," says Dose, "but for me, it was clear that they were a cut above the others in terms of artistic consistency." Speaking of Måneskin's sense of performance, Caffarelli recalls how they were the only band – counting all editions of the festival – that asked and were allowed to perform with two dancers on stage during the final live show. Galassi remembers the night he saw them at *Pulse*: "Technically speaking, it wasn't the best concert of Måneskin. But it was clear that they just had to achieve better coordination." After all, those were their first gigs.

Galassi went on to say:

> "However, they convey a lot, they gave a lot. They were very genuine guys, very energetic. Perhaps as for musical technique, they still had work to do if compared to other bands, in any case, their music was simple and straightforward... Yet, they had a very fresh sound, they had a sound that really rocked. The public liked them. I liked them a lot."

He liked them so much that he had a 'vision,' Galassi saw the light like John Belushi in *Blues Brothers* In fact, he wrote an article where he claimed to have: 'experienced a possible future of Italian music.' It was May 24, 2016. Måneskin had been together for six months, those were their first big gigs. Many readers, stopping on Galassi's article, must have thought: "He's giving too much credit to them!"

Yet, the prophetic Galassi reiterates in those few lines that, despite everything, despite the qualitative gap between Damiano and the others, despite the screams of the girls, mostly for Ethan (which, given Damiano's *coolness*, amazed the journalist himself – Ethan was not like today), something had happened on that stage. That said, he starts giving Måneskin good advice like an older brother. The band will follow some suggestions ("the producers will try to do anything to separate Damiano from the rest of the band" – yes, it happened, but Damiano didn't want to), and reject others ("insert electronic element" – everyone did it in that period).

This was the first article by a professional about the band.

At the end of the evening, Galassi wanted to meet Måneskin, he found them happy but above all amazed by what they had achieved. Davide Dose made them play during a Spaghetti Unplugged evening and in another small venue in the Roman district of Montesacro, the Comò Bistrot. The *Pulse* network gave good results for a while.

The band kept the name 'Måneskin,' initially thought of as temporary, it became a good luck charm after the *Pulse* victory. Måneskin wrote *Chosen* because the final stage of the contest required an original tune.

"We did a lot of bad, bad, bad gigs," said Damiano years later to Zach Sang, "but it was cool anyway."

On Galassi's website, attached to the famous article, there is also a video where Måneskin cover *Made*, a tune by DUB FX. An unexpected choice, the cover of a musician halfway between hip hop, pop, reggae, and electronic. After all, despite the wishes of Victoria and Thomas, Måneskin didn't start as a rock band. Moreover, the flow of DUB FX is not very easy to replicate, yet Damiano, on the rhythmic base of the others (the homemade recording amplifies the sound of Victoria), is pretty good at it. Besides, the Australian artist busked a lot as they will.

A long time ago, all bands started playing covers. The first Beatles records are full of covers. One cuts one's teeth learning the structures of songs written by others. The market started to crave original songs right from the start, around the seventies. Covers are a dimension that *X-Factor*, and talent shows at large, have brought back. About playing covers, Thomas Raggi told Zach Sang: "we try to experiment also a lot with the covers of some other artist 'cause it's very important for us...", Damiano completed the sentence, "...to put our signature on, kind of, everything." Måneskin, at this stage of their career, after *Pulse*, had few originals and many covers.

Playing in the streets

Måneskin started busking in Rome in via del Corso after *Pulse.* The contest encouraged the band, they began to put all their energy into setting out to make the right moves. Caffarelli asked to be the band's manager, but the band said no due to parental interventions, probably by Thomas's father. It was he, in fact, that later became the first manager of the band.

"We were in the square of the church of Santi Ambrogio and Carlo," Måneskin would later say to *Il Messaggero:* "next to the breakdancing group, we competed with the other street artists for the spots."

Interviewed at Eurovision, Damiano spoke about how the band was kind of forced to play on the streets in Rome, given the shortage of venues suitable for a rock band. "We decided to go onto the streets," he said, "because we basically needed money." Later, the singer explained to Zach Sang:

"We were kinda forced to because in Rome there are not like many, many places to play and nobody wants to pay you and it's kinda hard, so it was like obligatory to start playing in the streets. I think that our stage presence comes from playing in the streets because you don't have an actual audience: they are not there to listen to you, they are just walking around so you have to grab their attention and the real goal is to make them stay *longer* – not just for a song but, like, one, two, five, six songs 'cause that's the moment when they give you the money."

Busking in Italy, at least until the early 2000s, was something that musicians didn't really consider, it was almost perceived as degrading. The economic crisis led many venues to close, while some realities that create tourism with busking (Grafton Street in Dublin) served as a source of inspiration. Yet, the stiffening of some urban police regulations in terms of amplification and decibels, through the following years, led musicians to actual protests to have the possibility to work in the streets – it's a struggle, still only partially resolved. Rome, whose chaotic bureaucracy is notorious, has been offering spaces for busking, more or less, for a few years before Måneskin got together. Getting the permits in the beginning wasn't easy at all, and the *vigili* (the urban police) often fined buskers anyway.

This is what Vic said on the subject:

> "I think one of our first memories as a band is when we started to play together in the streets. At first, we were, like, sixteen years old and we went to this very noisy street in Rome and we just stayed there and played there until, like, the cops came for us."

Yes, it could happen to anyone, including those who respected urban regulations. It can still happen sometimes. Måneskin had a nemesis though, an old lady under whose balcony the band often played. It was she who regularly took the phone and called the urban police (via del Corso is also known as the *posh* street of Rome).

Yet, despite all the issues, busking is an extremely formative experience.

In Vic's words:

> "It was really nice, it really got us close and it made us even more friends than we were: we started to know each other and stand together even if it was a little bit tough at first,

but it helped us a lot to improve our stage presence too 'cause we had, like, to grab people's attention."

Anyone who has played on the streets knows what an irreplaceable testing ground it is, in terms of attracting the attention of people who are not there to listen to music. Thomas also said that: "It was necessary for practice, you know. And also, for problem-solving: you know, sometimes... I don't know, the strings of the guitar: ok, let's go on, the show must go on."

At Eurovision, Damiano described the street experience as follows:

"At the beginning, it's really embarrassing because you have to, like, take all your instruments in the middle of the street and put them right there and say 'ok, I am gonna play right now.'"

"And everyone is, like, hating you," added Vic, "the people that live there were always calling the police."

"And all the other street performers were like, 'mmm, that's my spot! '" concluded the singer.

On the streets, Thomas and Victoria were plugged into a small amp while Ethan was performing on the typical instrument of street drummers: the cajon. "Cajon" means "wooden box" in Spanish and that's exactly what it is: a percussion instrument box-shaped. Busking helped the band in terms of coordination, it also helped them to dismiss what Davide Dose calls 'the little sound,' and to capture their own unmistakable sound. "We played one hour and a half and we played, like, every day," said Damiano – even if from old Facebook posts it seems that Saturday was the day when it was more likely to meet Måneskin in the street. According to Damiano, their repertoire consisted of about thirty covers and two-three original tunes. If we look at the proportions between time and money, playing on the street paid more than clubs: "Those live shows were worth something, we were going strong: 50-100 euros per hour. Then sometimes there was the tourist or the sheik who left us 20 euros out of sympathy."

It's not easy to present a rock sound where you need to stay within certain volumes and where you can't bring the drums. The lack of places suitable for playing rock will be the first of a series of challenges for the band: everything led to suggest a change of sound, something lighter would have worked better on the market. So, early Måneskin were funky and white soul. Sometimes, they experimented with a hip hop or reggaeton voice on a rock-pop base.

With 'the box' (that's a term for street money) as Victoria recalls, the four paid for their first recordings on their own, a whole session paid with coins. The studio must have loved them so much for that.

The band is like a family

Playing together, like acting or being together in a writers' room, offers a chance to get to know new, intimate sides of co-authors. And if the basis is firm, a friendship grows stronger. A band becomes almost like a second family, this enhances the chemistry between its members – hence the quality of the performances. Måneskin proved that. Damiano spoke about this type of chemistry:

> "Growing up together helps you kind of set on the same path, but on the other hand, it's something that happens naturally. I think that the fact that we are very close friends helps the chemistry, because I think that if you take it as a job and – I don't know – you feel your bandmates are colleagues you cannot create this kind of chemistry. The band has to be like your family."

After the trip to Faenza to attend the MEI, Måneskin had a series of gigs including school parties (such as that of Liceo Virgilio, where Vic was still studying, at the venue *Sans Papiers*) and gigs around Rome (in a place on the Portuense hills called *Pozzo der Gelato*, at the *Cantine*, and at the Melting Pot event organized by a club named *Seedo*). Then other contests followed (the *Contestaccio* in March 2017), not to mention the continued busking. It's the standard path of every emerging band that wants to be heard, in short.

Acoustic rehearsals, on the other hand, were mainly done at Vic's home. Damiano David with his, definitely less rock approach to vocals (despite his love for Aerosmith and Guns N' Roses), had brought into the group a type of flow and a way of singing closer to Paolo Nutini with whom he has been compared to, so much so that Måneskin soon covered *New Shoes*. The intersection of these different dimensions, tested in this very period, is what immediately made recognizable some characteristics of their sound as 'Made in Måneskin,' like the almost rap vocal parts of a tune such as *Zitti e Buoni* or *Nel nome del padre.*

The first original song, that also came out with a video, was *Chosen*. The video was directed by Commando Creativo, two video makers who had heard Måneskin at *Pulse*. It's not the video that will be released later, during *X-Factor,* in which they perform the same song. Today the old YouTube link no longer works, probably due to exclusive rights. "One small step for humanity, one big step for Måneskin," Ethan commented wryly on Facebook when it was released.

A schoolmate interviewed Vic pretty much in those days for an internal newspaper, *School makes headlines* (La scuola fa notizia), at her high school. She described the genre of Måneskin as follows:

> "The genre we play... I don't really know how to describe it because we are attempting to create a fresh and new sound, I would say it includes different genres that we try to combine. We have some rap/hip hop, soul, R&B, blues, pop, and funky influences. I'm not sure how to describe it."

Indeed, in *Chosen* Damiano shows off his typical way of singing, perfectly suitable for upbeat songs, Thomas opposes it with a guitar which is definitely funky, supported by the solid backbone of Vic's bass. The tune came from Damiano's words and melodic line, arranged by the others: later the working method will vary depending on who has the clearest idea of a song. The lyrics talk about music and Måneskin themselves: plain and simple. There isn't much to guess.

"This is not music, this is life, this is what I live for" sings Damiano before launching the catchphrase: "follow me, follow me now." The front-man will describe *Chosen* after *X-Factor* as follows:

> "*Chosen* reflects, in a way, how our band has started, that is, from a casual but beautiful thing. That is: she took the bass, she played these... two notes, at the end and... it seemed cool to us, so we took it forward and out came a product that we are super proud of."

Radio Città Futura, a private radio based in Rome, interviewed Ethan, Thomas, and Damiano during the show *My Generation* the day before their gig at the Melting Pot event. It was called The Melting Pot because of the diverse types of music they mixed in a single evening. Presenting the band, Damiano defined it as: 'soul, pop, and hip hop.' Together with them on air (and lately on stage) was the twenty-five-year-old singer-songwriter Carlo Palermo and Virtus, a reggae/ragamuffin vocalist. The three boys – Damiano brought crutches as his ankle wasn't in a decent shape – gave a live acoustic performance of *Chosen* with the cajon and without the bass. Kevin Bonocore and Elisabetta Ranieri, the hosts, expressed their appreciation through selfies and standing ovations. Damiano was eighteen, Thomas had recently turned sixteen, Victoria (who wasn't there) would have turned seventeen the following month, and Ethan in October. Youth – associated with charisma – immediately jumped into everyone's view.

Ethan, who always looks cool and quiet, deceived Kevin Bonocore who fantasized about the possibility that, during a quarrel, the drummer might have been 'the peacemaker.' The other two were not so sure about that and instead, elected Thomas as 'the calmest.'

In perspective it's funny when Damiano improvises, explaining the meaning of Måneskin as moonlight: "A sense of peace that we wanted to express with our music, to be listened to on the sofa." It's hard to believe, but we love him anyway. Damiano himself, however, a few minutes later talks about his need to make music as a profession and, as the matter is serious, he turns brutally honest: "It's almost a forced-choice," he says, "it's this or nothing." It is something in which many creative minds by trade can easily identify.

Måneskin were, at the time, working on their first EP, they had written four out of five songs, two of which were in Italian. *Chosen*, as a single, was released on YouTube and other platforms. During the radio show, Damiano also announced an imminent departure for Copenhagen during the Easter holidays: Vic had stirred up her acquaintances for a few gigs outside Italy. After all, the band is like a big family and if one member wants to visit distant relatives, the other three will follow.

So, after *Contestaccio,* there were other gigs in Roman clubs such as the *Rashomon* in the Ostiense area and the *Big Star* in Trastevere. Then, it was time for Denmark: the gigs were at *Retro Café* and at *TijllyPop* in Copenhagen. From the beginning, Måneskin intended not to confine their music to Italy's borders. It could not be any other way for a band of musicians born at the turn of the millennium; part of a generation that takes the good sides of globalization for granted.

Especially for Damiano, as he declared to *Il Corriere della Sera*, after Denmark:

"That was the turning point, five days at home together, we never quarreled. We left it unsaid, yet we thought, 'fuck it works!'. After the trip to Denmark, rehearsals were one hour a day, then one hour turned to six, then eight, then twenty-four and we were always together."

Vic felt the same. In January 2018, she said that:

"One of my most important memories of Måneskin is when we went to Denmark, we lived together and played every day. There we understood that we were made to be together. That's where Måneskin was actually born, we understood that this was what we really wanted to do in our lives and that we were ready to take it all. "

The first time the band started talking about outfits was in Copenhagen, after a foray – the first of a series – into various second-hand clothing stores. From Denmark, they kept recording and posting covers on social media. The first one, on the Jamaican side of Måneskin, is *Road to Zion* by Damian Marley (son of Bob) in which Damiano inserts some rap lines in Italian. The second cover is *What they want* by Russ, a trap tune raised in tone and turned into an unplugged white soul tune. The third song belongs to, once again, trap music: *Trankilo* by Vegas Jones (who, despite his stage name, is Italian and will later collaborate with Måneskin). In this song, Damiano's lightning-fast flow takes the listener's breath away – literally. It's all sung without autotune.
Trap music – In Puerto-Rican style adapted to Italian – Is very popular, as you can guess.
Considering the list of gigs and venues so far, it's clear how Måneskin lived and dealt with music, keeping a regularity in

rehearsals and live shows. That's what it takes to make a profession out of it.

Back from Denmark, Måneskin regained their spot on via del Corso. They now had a Facebook page that had reached 2000 likes in April 2017, the day after Vic's birthday. They opened their Instagram page in May, Ethan opened his personal one in June. Chiara Iannotta filmed them near the Geox shop in via del Corso. They played *Ragamuffin* by Selah Sue. The famous picture of Måneskin playing on the street that circulated on social networks after they won Sanremo is taken from this session.

In another video of that period, Damiano gives a scratchy and suffered version of *Back to Black* by Amy Winehouse in which Vic plays the acoustic bass. It is always the same photographer, Chiara Iannotta, who takes the pictures for the first official book of the band: the ones where Ethan reads *The book of photography in color*, where Vic has a beer in her hand and sits in an armchair (which, in another shot, she gives up for Damiano), where Damiano is behind her and Thomas is pensively staring at his phone. Probably, *Zitti e Buoni* was already in the air, since the bassist wrote on May 7, 2017, on her Facebook page: "We are out of our minds, but different from them." ("*siamo fuori di testa, ma diversi da loro*") No song, no video, just this.

In May 2017, the band is ready for the release of the video and single of *Recovery*, their second original tune. It came out after a gig at *BertaniDai* and one at *Villaggio Globale*, on June 8, 2017. Chiara Iannotta, once again, also directed *Recovery*'s video, the song is definitely upbeat and good for dancing. The concept of the video is a satire on rockstars and their decadence. In retrospect, it's awkward seeing Damiano naked in the tub without his tattoos, while a kiss with Vic shocked his early days fans. The bass player, holding her dog Chili, plays the part of a posh lady. Ethan gets his sandals polished, but he wears socks underneath them and that's rather funny. Thomas's sequence is also funny as he has slaves waving palm leaves over him. In a few years, the scene of fans trying to get pieces of the four Måneskin members will come true. An Instagram user writes below the video: "From a thirty-year-old who grew up listening to great voices in a tape player, I can tell you that I hope you'll get so far that you can't figure how (it bothers me to tell you this, as you are an eighteen-year-old, but you're a great front-man)."

On June 12, 2017, *X-Factor* is mentioned for the first time on Måneskin's social networks.

Part 3.

The second place at X-Factor Italy

Before X-Factor

A ccording to Victoria De Angelis:
"We weren't even sure we wanted to go there; I mean to X-Factor. The reason? The way television programs are perceived. People often think it's all fake there. But eventually, we accepted: it was a way to share our music with a larger audience."

And that is true, it's undeniable.
What else is true, is that in some music schools, they recommend that you not participate in talent shows – or if it is the case, it's best that you don't win – to be able to manage contracts by yourself. On the other hand, it's also true that nowadays *X-Factor* is one of the few opportunities to hear emerging music on television, bypassing social media and reaching the non-native technological generations.
Måneskin passed the first selection. Meanwhile, they kept doing gigs in Rome (*Chiringuito, Bibliotechina*). They were also chosen as an opening act in a concert at *Roma Village*

where the headliners were the Daiana Lou, a duo of buskers that had participated in *X-Factor* 2016.

Then came their cover of a famous song by Caparezza, an Italian rapper halfway between conscious and alternative hip hop, famous for his sharp irony. *Vieni a ballare in Puglia* (*Come to dance in Puglia*, which Måneskin ragamuffined – the original rhythm is tarantella-like) is a protest song easily mistaken for a light, danceable tune. It talks about how the careless tourist on holiday in the Puglia region, the heel of Italy, does not notice the deadly dioxin released in Taranto by the Ilva steel mills, or the summer bonfires on the massif of Gargano – meanwhile, all those businessmen who caused all those damages around think: "that the Kyoto protocol is a Japanese erotic film." Caparezza is one of the non-rock influences of the band, Vic and Ethan saw him in concert during the same gig, at the Capannelle hippodrome, Rome. It wasn't until 2021, during a *Rockol* interview, the drummer and the bassist found out that they had both been there.

All through the summer of 2017, the band kept announcing that they had really big news at stake that could not be revealed from their social networks. They released another video, a cover this time by the Black Eyed Peas – *Let's Get it Started* – to which Damiano added a bit in Italian which is almost a monologue. In August, the band was finally featured on Spotify.

From all these new pictures, these videos released one after the other, this 'saying' without really talking about the big news to come, it's easy to guess that meanwhile, the band was passing the various selections of *X-Factor*: the "On the road" phase, the castings, then the auditions that were held in Pesaro on June 12, 2017 – that same day they mentioned the name of the talent show for the first time on their Facebook page. The auditions before the judges were on September 21. The song that Måneskin performed, their first on TV, was *Chosen* – the arrangement was definitely more rock than the funky vibe of their first recordings. The judges of that edition of *X-Factor* were the singer-songwriter Levante, the rapper Fedez (rapper and husband of the Milanese influencer Chiara Ferragni), the music talent scout Mara Maionchi and Manuel Agnelli, front-man of the all-Italian rock band Afterhours. Måneskin finally convinced them and moved to the next round.

At the Bootcamps, the band performed another song by Caparezza, *Io vengo dalla luna* (*I come from the moon*) – dismissing ragamuffin for a more rock-ish tone. They were in Manuel Agnelli's hands, it was he who decided the fate of the bands. On the other hand, Levante was dancing, absorbed by their music. They had their chair. On to the next round.

Manuel Agnelli and the Afterhours

*I didn't choose music to play the music I wanted;
I choose music to live as I wanted. It's a bit different.*
[Manuel Agnelli]

Manuel Agnelli (we would write Añelli, if he were Spanish) is a key figure in this story, so we need to make a small digression on the history of his band – Afterhours – and on his relevance in the Italian rock scene of the nineties.

Born in 1966, Agnelli founded the band at the age of twenty in 1986. 1986, if compared to the time of Måneskin, was another world, another scene, another city: Milan, the other big city of Italy, the opposite pole of Rome. Afterhours sang their first record in English since their references were in the New York scene of the seventies: Lou Reed and Television on the top of the list. From the very beginning, their sound was rough, disturbed, suffered: Afterhours were (and still are) alternative rock. There used to be an important contest in Italy, called Arezzo Wave. It was for a themed compilation linked to that contest that Afterhours sang for the first time in Italian. The theme was: songs by Rino Gaetano, an important singer-songwriter from the late seventies, who died prematurely in a car accident.
Another cover (*La canzone popolare*) made by Afterhours was also crucial in making the band turn to Italian, they released it for a tribute album to a living singer-songwriter this time: Ivano Fossati. Years later, Manuel will recognize Fossati's influence in his first lyrics in Italian. From that moment on – we are in the early nineties – Afterhours

definitively dismissed English, moving towards a way of writing between sarcasm and advertising slogans, between sufferance and sensuality. The breakthrough album was *Germi,* it was 1995.

An important singer, almost a mother for Italian pop music, Mina (aged 55), liked the record. Retired from the scene since 1978, Mina hasn't appeared in public since the late seventies. She is always up-to-date though, with the underground scene of Milan and Italy in general (today, even at eighty-two, she doesn't dislike rap, trap, or electronics). She is also a discoverer of talents, it was her version of *La canzone di Marinella* (*Marinella's song*) that launched Fabrizio De André, now considered one of the greatest Italian songwriters, the likes of Leonard Cohen (that he translated and covered in Italian). Anyway, Mina sang a song from *Germi, Dentro Marylin* (*Inside Marylin*) changing the title to *Tre volte dentro me* (*Three times inside me*). For Afterhours, that was a turning point. The following year, they released their second album in Italian, *Hai paura del buio?* (*Are you afraid of the dark?*), a must in their discography.

But Manuel Agnelli, who at the time had long black, straight hair like Ethan, is not just a musician. Given that the Italian alternative scene – which has always been rich, and still is, with interesting experiences and sounds – was not really considered by majors, Agnelli invented a festival with the collaboration of the record company under which the Afterhours released their records at the time, Mescal. The *Tora! Tora!* Festival created a network between the major labels and songwriters such as Cristina Donà (her first album, *Tregua, Ceasefire*, was produced by Agnelli), or new bands such as Subsonica, Linea 77, and Marlene Kuntz. Other important bands that stood out at the festival were Verdena (alt-rock), Modena City Ramblers (Irish folk),

Shandon (punk, ska), and Massimo Volume (post-rock). The *Tora! Tora!* ended when the collaboration between Afterhours and Mescal finished. Yet, it left its mark.

"If there's one thing I'm sorry about," Manuel told Cesare Basile years later, "it is when I see talented people that don't have the means to do what they want."

Let's jump from 2005 to 2016. This metamorphosis of Agnelli – from a key figure of the Italian underground to judge on *X-Factor* – a judge with a stern and provocative artistic persona, sometimes mean, often brutally sincere – disoriented the old fan base a little. In Italy, especially in Manuel's generation, rock is deeply linked to counterculture. For many, it's good, perhaps, that it doesn't mix with *mainstream* so as not to turn into a sell-out genre, so as not to be tamed. Many members of the Italian hip hop underground of the nineties also made their musical choices following this philosophy. As Manuel himself said, "We still had a certain type of cultural structure – questionable or not – which led us to have opinions that did not depend on numbers. They did not depend on success and results."

Yet, Manuel Agnelli, with his incredible musical competence, his smart pragmatism, and adding a good dose of *poker face*, chose to go on TV and to become one of the faces of *X-Factor Italy*. It took him a year to make up his mind, his first edition as a judge was that of 2016.
Working on television, he realized that not only the careless boomers but also millennials, the target audiences of certain TV shows, didn't know a thing about the Italian underground scene. So, his thirty-year-long honorable career went unnoticed – as they were not under the spotlight. Indeed,

Manuel Agnelli has always had – since the days of *Tora! Tora!* – the desire and the intention to give space to the actual music of the moment, helping remarkable projects make their way in a market, often a slave of trends, where one has to push hard to pass. Probably he decided to be part of such an important talent show because, deep down in his artistic history, this wish not to "chase what is happening but nurture what will happen" has always been there. *X-Factor* led him into the control room, so much so that he had such visibility in return that he was able to reinvest his new popularity in other projects, such as festivals, to spread his, 'point of view.'

Cultural responsibility is something that Agnelli always took on, despite fears and concerns. In fact, he confessed to *Rolling Stone Italia* that on his first X Factor season he was kind of scared of facing: "something that seemed very far from me," not to mention the awkwardness of some embarrassing moments, such as X-Factor's red carpet ("The other three judges signed autographs and shook hands and I didn't know what the fuck I could do because no one in the audience gave a shit about me.").

He also spoke about being part of X-Factor over the course of the program *La confessione (The confession)* hosted by journalist Peter Gomez:

> "I actually entered *X-Factor* for many reasons: some of those are vulgar such as visibility, work, and the possibility of carrying out projects that I am actually working on, others are nobler such as being able to pull the show away from trash, focusing it on music."

That's the same principle behind the two seasons of the TV program conceived by Manuel Agnelli for the public broadcasting channel, Rai 3: *Ossigeno* (*Oxygen*). If on *X-Factor* Manuel aimed to have the pulse of the future musical scene, *Ossigeno* has managed to bring music back into broadcasting, in non-talent show contexts. "For me, it is important to occupy cultural spaces that open up," he told *Rolling Stone Italy*, "We always complain that there is never anything on television, there is never a vision of things that look like ours... and then in the end, when we have the opportunity to bring it in on a TV show, we give up out of... fear, because this is the truth." In hosting *Ossigeno*, Agnelli used the old *catchphrase* of Chevy Chase on Saturday Night Live: "I am Manuel Agnelli and you are not." That tells you something about his personality, how he mixes irony with his dark image as the Severus Snape of rock and roll.

He is also persuaded that a band is 'a group of friends who share the same things.'

In 2021, he expressed his opinion on Måneskin:

> "First of all, there are pharisees who hold the truth about what rock and roll is and what is not rock and roll, I would like to understand who gave them this degree because, more often than not, they are not rock and roll at all. Having said that, if you compare Måneskin to Sonic Youth you don't understand shit about Måneskin. Måneskin are a mainstream group: you can compare them to Aerosmith, to InXs. They always have wanted to be a mainstream group. The key to interpreting Måneskin is their freshness, their personality, their innate performative talent and the fact that they currently represent the present."

Back to September 2017. Manuel Agnelli listened to Måneskin during the auditions. Of the four judges (and the audience, which gave a standing ovation), he was the least impressed. Talent scout Mara Maionchi – who began by asking: "How many years ago were you in middle school?" – seemed the most convinced. Her only doubt concerned singing in English, as she thought it would lead the band to sell less. Rapper Fedez instead was struck by Damiano, while Levante found a slight lack of coordination still there – nothing serious, though. While these three gave a positive response out of gut instinct, Manuel Agnelli was enumerating in his head the weaknesses of the band: the lack of coordination was still evident, so was the presence of a member that needed to study more than the others – Ethan. "You are still very raw," said he, freezing them. "We are ready to work hard," replied Damiano. "I am not sure that you can do the hard work you need in a very short time, this is my only doubt," Agnelli retorted, "yet, there's something in there."

So, the Afterhours front-man finally said yes, but when the band left the stage, he kept expressing his doubts to Mara Maionchi: "A band, indeed they are. But, can I say something? The drummer is terrible and that's what slows down everything." On this point, Levante agreed. Manuel Agnelli then asked a direct question to Mara Maionchi: "Would you take them in your team?" Without batting an eye, the talent scout replied: "Yes, absolutely."

Manuel was full of doubts. He will have time to change his mind.

X-Factor 2017

Rockstars are born, not made.
[Vic]

At the Judges' homes in Manchester, in October 2017, Manuel Agnelli listened to Måneskin together with Skin, lead vocalist of Skunk Anansie. He chose the song *You Need Me and I Don't Need You* by Ed Sheeran for them. Ethan wore his hair in pigtails for the occasion.

They passed on to the next stage – Live Show one – together with another rock band: Ros, characterized by a rock-punk sound and the fuchsia hair of the singer and guitarist Camilla Giannelli. Måneskin thus officially entered the core of the competition. They announced it on social media on October 19, 2017. The short video in which they introduced the band for the show was released on October 26.

In the first video-diary, Vic tries not to be on camera as she is disheveled and she is not wearing make-up. Actually, no one wears any and the whole band has messy hair: it had been backcombed for a video, part of the scenography for the song from the first live show. They mention Luca Tommassini, the choreographer who apparently conceived the scenography. Although "here [in the loft of *X-Factor*] we freak out," Damiano immediately declares himself as the most nervous, the band is in good hands: Rodrigo D'Erasmo is taking care of the bands. D'Erasmo is a multi-instrumentalist with more than twenty years of experience (he played the intro of *Survival* by Muse, among other things). He is also part of Afterhours since 2008 and, in a way, he is a sort of right-hand man to Manuel Agnelli.

Still, in the video, Thomas says he liked the last rehearsals – supervised by D'Erasmo. Then the band makes a list of friends with whom they socialized: first Lorenzo Bonamano – La Bonnie – then the singer-songwriter Enrico Nigiotti ('a legend'), Virginia Perbellini – La Perbe – the electro-pop duo Sem & Stènn and Ros who, as a band, are on the same team as theirs. Finally, Damiano confesses that he has not been drinking for ten days – it is forbidden by regulation.

What Måneskin do not say in the video is that in the beginning with Tommassini it was certainly not simple. The choreographer has an outstanding CV that includes (among others) Geri Halliwell, Kylie Minogue, Katy Perry... His dancer CV is even scarier: there are names like Madonna (*Girlie Show*, 1993), Diana Ross (Super Bowl XXX), Prince, Janet Jackson, Whitney Houston, again Kylie Minogue, Michael Jackson (*Blood on the Dance floor*, 1997) ... In short, Luca Tommassini is a top player, the best the contestants of *X-Factor* can get. Yet, he himself will tell the press years later that the first impact with Måneskin was tough:

"They didn't want to go on stage, they refused my staging. I was amazed. I thought I was the star of the show. The others told me: "Give them a lesson," instead I asked to speak to them. When I saw them walking, I immediately had the feeling that they were stars. I asked what the problem was and they – they were very young at the time – gave me a nice speech: "We are all together, we have seen, studied, heard what we need, we have a project and we want to stage exactly what we are. Whatever you have thought will not be in line with this." And for the first time, I agreed to design the 'mise-en-scène' together with the artists. Never done before. I changed my method thanks to these phenomenal young guys."

Tommassini is not a fool, he accepted the challenge by working side by side with the band that, do not forget, had existed for less than two years.

"I proposed solutions using my know-how, my team. I was trying to create a 'style' that they could feel was their own, I was trying to make them glam while keeping their identity intact. They didn't have the tools to stage themselves as they would have liked and they took the opportunity to take advantage of me."

Luca Tommassini is, therefore, the first to put on scene the self-staging fantasies of Måneskin. Still, they conceived the style of their performances together. Years later, he will remember the four like this:

"They had already seen the world through smartphones and the Internet, while we needed a plane. I used the stage to show how they were, I wanted to shed light better on what they already had inside, I made what they had theatrical, explosive. XF was their testing ground, but they seemed born for that."

About the meetings with Måneskin, he said: "They did not last long, there was honesty and truth in what they said. They did not try to justify what they wanted to do: they strongly supported their ideas. And every meeting ended with Victoria saying, 'fuck, yeah'."

Vic at the time (like the whole band) flaunted her *"coatto"'* identity.

How could I explain the concept of *"coatto"* (plural, *coatti;* feminine *coatta/e*) to those who do not know Rome? It's a term that during *X-Factor* is often mentioned by the band. In Italy, there is a whole imagery centered on the 'coatti of Rome.' It starts with comedies like *Gallo Cedrone (Grouse)* by Carlo Verdone and passes through some cult songs like *Supercafone (Superjerk)* by rapper Piotta. In Italian, *"coatto"* means 'forced, compulsory.' In Rome instead, *coatto* is someone proudly rough who speaks and dresses vulgarly and acts over the top. The main character of *Gallo Cedrone*, for example, drives a massive motorcycle and dresses up like Elvis, of which he believed he is the illegitimate son. In general, *coatti* belong to a low social class (the term itself betrays class prejudices). As for Måneskin, they are not lower class, yet they used the term reclaiming their belonging (Rome), boosting those *coattos* characteristics in line with the aggressiveness of their music. Later, Damiano will declare, once out of *X-Factor*: "When we got on stage, we already had the reputation of being unpleasant, we are 'coatti' because the *coatti* have the arrogance, the irreverence that makes them fearless in facing the elders. We are common teenagers who felt trapped in their teenage life."

During one of the *dailies* dated November 21, Damiano gives *coatto* dress-code lessons to the other contestants: Nigiotti had to wear the collar of his coat high, Gabriele Esposito had to open his shirt showing his chest. In the same video, Vic gives *coatto* make-up lessons: five wipes of bronzer on the face.

2017 was the eleventh season of *X-Factor* Italy. The first Live Show was opened by the Ibeyi as special guests. Måneskin followed soon after with their cover of *Let's get it started* by the Black Eyed Peas, the right track to kick it off with a burst of energy. As Damiano jumped onto the judges' table, Fedez seemed to like the performance. To make up for his comments about the "terrible drummer" at the auditions, Manuel Agnelli wanted to underline that: "Ethan has freakishly improved as a drummer in a very short time." On the same evening, with a wholly different musical genre, Enrico Nigiotti also stood out. He is a singer-songwriter from Leghorn who had a previous experience with judge Maionchi: the production of a record that he quit halfway through. X-Factor was not his first talent show, as he had also taken part in the already mentioned all-Italian *Amici*. That evening, Nigiotti sang *La chanson des vieux amants* (*Song of Old Lovers*) by Jacques Brel in Italian, and the vulnerability that the song brought out of him made a sharp contrast to his macho tanned appearance. Given that Agnelli, the judge of the bands, had expressed doubts about the choice of the song, Mara Maionchi, the judge of the over twenty-fives, which included Nigiotti, commented combatively that the tune is difficult to sing. Then she added, referring to Damiano: "Much easier to move your ass and make a mess jumping on a table – way much easier! I have seen a lot of messes on tables!"

In the video-diary that follows, Damiano commented: "The judges' table is very slippery, guys, don't go up there because I seriously risked falling... on Maionchi, shit! Poor thing!"

It's clear from the beginning that the band must watch out for Nigiotti, and Samuel Storm, a nineteen-year-old Sicilian-Nigerian whose execution of *Location* by Khalid was so perfect that Fedez blurts out: "Guys, is there any shit you have to tell Samuel at all?" And above all, Lorenzo Licitra, a half-tenor, half-crooner with a beautiful voice that he showed on the first live show, performing *Your Song*.

Instead, the judges are doubtful about Bonamano, whose interpretation of *High Hopes* goes into the ballot with *Adam's Song* by Blink 182 remade by guitarist Gabriele Esposito. During the ballot, Bonamano performed *Radioactive* by Imagine Dragons and Gabriele Esposito *Ain't No Sunshine* by Bill Whiters – Esposito made it through.

In the video-diaries that follow, many will complain about the absence of Lorenzo Bonamano, 'La Bonnie,' in the loft. Gabriele Esposito is the first to call him "the soul of the loft" and, in his video message, he is very sad. Damiano comments: "Unfortunately Bonnie has been kicked off." "...and Damiano and I cried more than Perbe [llini] and Rita [Bellanza, another contestant] put together," said Vic, "We will no longer cry like this for any of the other contestants" continues Damiano. What follows is a sweet kind of teasing, at the end of which Vic tells the camera – and it seems like they are not in the loft of *X-Factor* but on a great school trip – that a few days earlier she and Damiano had slipped an egg into Bonamano's shoe, thinking that the victim would soon put them on, breaking it. "But he didn't put his shoes on for four days, then he packed them, then he went back... home, I think, and so, he'll have his whole suitcase full of cracked eggs," says Vic. Bonamano himself joked a lot: in his first video message he throws lemons at Virginia Perbellini while Camille Cabaltera (from women under twenty-five) says in her video message that Bonamano awakened her from naps on the sofa by throwing water in her face.

Back to Måneskin's second video-diary. As for the music, the band also reveals that Rodrigo D'Erasmo has assigned them their second live song. Then the band, together with Samuel Storm, invades the video message of Ros. Altogether, they sing an old rock and roll tune, *Svalutation* (*Devaluation*) by Adriano Celentano, commenting "Yeah, we like it rough."

On the second Live Show, the guest star is Sam Smith who opens the evening with *Stay with me*. Dua Lipa follows with *New Rules*. The first of the contestants to sing is Nigiotti, staging a pop-rock version of a rap song by the most famous member of old school Italian conscious hip hop, Frankie hi-nrg. The song is *Quelli che benpensano* (*Those who think-right*) and it does not impress Fedez, the judge that comes from hip hop culture, but the others like it: Nigiotti becomes even more menacing and earns a good score. On the other hand, Lorenzo Licitra unleashes his tenor voice staging *Miserere* by Zucchero and Pavarotti. Tough round.

As for Måneskin, their song is *Beggin'*. It was 2017. That's why – and Måneskin often mention this during interviews – it is weird that the song achieved international success in 2021 given that it has been around for four long years. The theme of the scenography has to do with the sea: on the stage, there is a sort of whale, while behind the band, there are videos shot in a swimming pool by the four Måneskin members and coordinated by Luca Tommassini. During the *dailies*, the making of the videos has been filmed, and there's Vic, teasing Ethan by saying: "In addition to being a terrible drummer, he is also terrible at diving."

Wearing a Johnny Depp –Mad-Hatter outfit, Damiano sang, perhaps in a slightly harsher way if compared to nowadays. The raucous feeling is perceivable when he closes some musical phrases – it's all in the details. Meanwhile on stage, Thomas has fun breaking the fourth wall and ventures into the audience. On his side of the jury, Manuel Agnelli laughs, happy about the performance. Judge Levante looks at the stage enraptured and judge Fedez praises the choice of song, appropriate for the sound and mood of the band. A choice that will pay off many years later – but this, the band could not have known.

It's now time for the singer Virginia Perbellini to leave, who fails on *The Dog Days are Over* from Florence and the Machine – her version, according to Agnelli, lacked charisma. She clashes with Ros, whose *Fiori d'arancio (Orange Flowers),* by the singer-songwriter Carmen Consoli, was maybe a bit too punk. Between *I Rise up* by Andra Day and a rusty reinterpretation of *Svalutation* by Celentano, Ros keep their place in the contest.

In the video-diary that follows, the one in which Thomas tries to be serious, but is sabotaged by Damiano and Vic, and in which they reveal their next cover, the four speak up about some secret details concerning life in the loft: Virginia Perbellini, 'La Perbellona,' according to Thomas (self-appointed cook of the house, together with Licitra): "was the only one who cleaned, while Gabriele Esposito doesn't do shit." Vic then, since the band has no contact with the outside world except through traditional mail, bursts out in one of her moments of brutal honesty:

> "We are like super-unlucky here at *X-Factor* because after every live show all the fucking contestants get like a hundred letters, a thousand cards and Licitra gets ten cartloads of food: I get nothing! Dad, you are an asshole! I say, nothing, not even a note – they had at least a note!"

"I got a razor," replies Thomas, "so uhm, I don't know what to say."

Then the 'trend' of imitating Levante and her way of talking starts, especially the way she uses the word 'diamonds' to describe shining performers. There is an indoor contest and, according to Vic, for now, the best impression of Levante is Enrico Nigiotti's. "But I can make a Samuel Storm impression," replies Damiano and proves it, revealing the singer's favorite pizza ("Capricciosa, double ham, without artichoke"). Vic makes a call to action: "send that pizza to Samuel to make him happy."

In the video-diary of Camilla (Ros) and Camille, Thomas 'Er Cobbra' shows off a rather impressive falsetto. He also sneaks into Gabriele Esposito's video.

As life in the loft is dull, they declare that there's a 'super-jokes dream team' including them and two supposed adults – the pizza chef and soul singer Andrea Radice and Nigiotti. They aim to animate the place during the moments of pause. Vic also slips into the same video (to say that Thomas doesn't clean much either) and finally, we have Damiano with his hair all over the place, whispering like a zombie: "Hi assholes" to the camera.

Meanwhile, Virginia Perbellini, in her farewell video, surprisingly guesses the three contestants that will gain the podium.

X-Factor is a huge contest that includes smaller challenges like Asus Unplugged. Here the prize is – needless to say – an unplugged recording sponsored by the tec company Asus. In order to gain votes, three out of four Måneskin members, with Enrico Nigiotti – Vic was ill then – put on an unplugged version of *Take me out* by Franz Ferdinand.

During the third live show, in which the guests are two stars that started on *X-Factor* (Harry Styles and the all-Italian star Michele Bravi), Nigiotti got a good score again, staging a 2002 protest song by a singer-songwriter we've already mentioned, Daniele Silvestri. The song is called *Il mio nemico* (*My enemy*), Silvestri is also the author of *Salirò*, the first tune ever heard by Damiano. Andrea Radice also impresses the jury with *I Need a Dollar*. Fedez is probably wrong when he tells Licitra and Nigiotti that it looks like they belong to another generation, Licitra looks old, Nigiotti sings 'old stuff.' He is surely wrong about Nigiotti's song; as later, post-covid, Silvestri himself, featuring the rapper Rancore, released *Il mio nemico* once again to talk about putting the blame on neighbors during the pandemic. A feeling very pushed by the media. The electro-pop duo Sem&Stènn does not impress with their 'orgy' (Maionchi) version of *Electric Feel* by MGMT and they impress even less with *This is Not a Love Song* by Public Image Limited. They are out.

What about Måneskin then? They can surely perform sybaritically better than Sem&Stènn. The song staged is *Somebody told me* by the Killers, once again the choice is perfect in terms of sound and lyrics. The stage (courtesy of Tommassini) turns black, white, and red emphasizing the red of Damiano's vest and Vic's lipstick. The bass player has very curly hair while the front-man has super tight pants. This time Fedez is right: "Three inches above all the performances we've heard – and I shouldn't say that" (since he had the male under-twenty-five category).

Måneskin won the Asus Unplugged challenge. In the fourth video-diary, Damiano immediately starts by saying: "Thank you dear audience, in addition to sending us very promiscuous and vulgar audio messages, you have voted and overwhelmed us." The song they chose to record is *Somebody told me* with "Enrico Nigiotti, that *coatto*!" on the second acoustic guitar. "*Coatti* hang out with other *coatti*," comments Vic. The version is still present on platforms and YouTube.

The band then reveals the following song and how it will sound (with a little help from Rodrigo D'Erasmo). Then they stop chatting about the previous performance. "Cool for Federi'!" Says Damiano addressing Fedez (street name of Federico Lucia) "we kicked the shit out of your contestants eh." Thomas says he feels sorry for Sem&Stènn, who were: "Among other things, part of those who cleaned the house." Concerning everyday life in the loft, the four all agree that among what's fun in there, 'insulting Esposito' is surely at the top of the list. "You don't have to insult him offensively," explains Damiano, "but in a nice way – yet, *do* insult him: call him names in many fancy ways then we will choose the term we like best and I'll get that tattooed on me." The whole loft was kind of annoyed by Gabriele Esposito because he was always singing, so much that his voice gets into the video message of the singer Rita Bellanza, making her blurt out: "Gabriele, I can't take it anymore!" After all, Måneskin launched the hashtag #espositoshutyourfuckingmouth.

At Live show number four the special guests, in addition to the famous singer and Facebook star Gianni Morandi, are Afterhours themselves – so maybe the *X-Factor* target audience will finally get to know their songs reassuring judge Agnelli. Afterhours perform *Bianca*.

In the lead positions, there are once again Nigiotti and Licitra. Nigiotti sings and plays *Make you Feel My Love* by Bob Dylan, Licitra has to deal with something apparently far away from his style, *Nothing Else Matters* by Metallica. The result is unexpectedly good. Camille Cabaltera incredibly doesn't impress the jury with her version of *Sorry Not Sorry* by Demi Lovato. She will not make it through the play-off against Gabriele Esposito, who sings and plays *The Man Who Can't Be Moved* by the Scripts (Camille brought *Bang Bang* by Jesse J, Ariana Grande, and Nicki Minaj).

Manuel Agnelli had chosen a daring piece for Måneskin: it was *Un temporale* (*A storm*) by soul singer, rapper, and songwriter Ghemon, a song released just a few months earlier. In the Måneskin version, the voice and arrangements are perhaps richer than the original. The performance takes place inside a net that's like a cloud, there are lights behind that imitate the lightning of a storm. Damiano exhibits his best soul voice, Vic looks like a blonde Morticia Adams in her long black dress with a vertiginous slit. Perhaps Thomas's intervention at the end of the song is not too bold – again, it's all in the details. Judge Levante tells Måneskin that they are: "My favorite diamonds after my girls." (Levante had women under 25.)

In the fifth video-diary, Måneskin keep being likable rogues, confessing that they have stolen the best room of the loft that the under-twenty-fives women wanted for themselves. But then, laughing and joking, Damiano confesses that *Un Temporale* by Ghemon did not start well: "Basically that song had a sort of curse because the day before we rehearsed, we messed it all up, I went crazy. Which actually never happens" (Ethan: "Nooo!") "So, I was shitting my pants when I performed it, I was shitting my pants on *X-Factor* for the first time." Vic adds:

> "But then when we finished, we went up and Manuel started to say [imitating him] "Guys, stay calm, whatever happens, you stay calm. The important thing is that you have given it your all" like one of those speeches you make to those who are out of the contest. And we were like "Oh, what the fuck!" that it, I was dying to go to sleep, "but why?"

But then the band passed through the turn and everything fell into place.
 "When we came back, he told me 'You're badly good'," adds Damiano on Manuel Agnelli, "I'm still looking for the meaning of this phrase." Victoria once again scolds her dad. He hasn't sent her anything again, after a note and 'an envelope full of junk food.' "My mother," replies Damiano, "who is a real *coatta*, sent me rings and necklaces." Finally, the band speaks up on Camille's defeat. "She was my pupil," Vic says, giving herself credit, together with Sem of Sem&Stènn, for having taught Camille how to turn away from a style that was all pianos and chastity.
 The next live show is going to be the one in which original songs are performed, so Vic guarantees that they will show everyone who the real *coatti* are "Because we come from Roma, yeah!" No trivia about *Chosen,* because 'trivia is for losers.' Yet, Ethan says that, when they recorded *Chosen,* Damiano had a forty-degree fever (104 F°). Rather common, right? Who hasn't recorded a song with a forty-degree fever? Thomas Er Cobbra keeps sneaking into others' videos, this time showing his earring in Andrea Radice's. Meanwhile,

Enrico Nigiotti complains that Er Cobbra has broken a string on his guitar.

So here we are. It's episode number five, the night of the unreleased songs. Competing with Måneskin are, Enrico Nigiotti, the tenor-crooner Lorenzo Licitra, the pizza chef and soul singer Andrea Radice, the annoying guitarist Gabriele Esposito, Ros, Samuel Storm and the singer Rita Bellanza. Three of them at least (Ros, Esposito and Nigiotti) had declared in their video-messages that, so far, their aim has been to stay on the show until that very evening. All the competitors, when the show opens, sing along with the popular band Negramaro.

During the first part of the show, contestants present their original songs, the second part is themed: 'Top Seller Artists.' Everyone among the competitors writes songs except Lorenzo Licitra, who shows up with a piece written for him by Fortunato Zampaglione (a famous lyricist, not a relative of Federico Zampaglione leader of the Tiromancino band) and Rita Bellanza who brings a song written by her judge, Levante. Måneskin present *Chosen* and, while playing it, they interact with the audience. Their performance is a cut above the rest. This time they win over everyone, including Licitra (who scores a 13.99% preference) and Nigiotti (who scores a 16.84% preference against a 24, 16% of Måneskin). Even Mara Maionchi takes back what she said on the first episode, the *moving-ass-on-tables* thing, commenting: "It is impossible for you to lose it, you are very tough, I am telling you that, you are very tough."
And, to make everything even better, Måneskin also win the second part of the show with *Take me out* by Franz Ferdinand. Only Nigiotti comes close to their score with

L'isola che non c'è (Neverland) by the Neapolitan singer-songwriter Edoardo Bennato. Gabriele Esposito fails against Samuel Storm, who was absolutely in his natural territory with *Rolling in The Deep* by Adele. The annoying guitarist then clashes with Rita Bellanza and his version of Adele's *When We Were Young* does not impress the jury. He is out.

On the sixth video-diary, Måneskin are ready to perform in an event sponsored by X-Factor, but they are last in the lineup ("But the last will be the first as Jesus said!" says Vic, "Cool for Jesus!" answer the others). This does not prevent them from talking about – what else –Esposito being out of the show: "And this is sad, but it's also happy," says Vic, "everything has changed, I swear, the loft is silent, everything is clean..." In his last video, Esposito said that, even if they joked and said 'ah you always sing', the others sang with him and, despite the *coatto*-attitude of Måneskin or the sharp jokes of Camilla from Ros, he was on good terms with everybody.
Vic then reveals that, in the next episode, they will start slowly 'then we'll turn on the *coattizer*!'

Måneskin keep intruding into video messages of the others, although there are fewer people in the loft: this time it is not Ethan but Damiano who plays the fool behind Ros's sofa.

The sixth is the third to last live show. The special guest, who enjoys flirting with Mara Maionchi, is Noel Gallagher. Ros will say: "He was lucky enough to open for Ros because we played immediately after him." Then Camilla tells the audience that before they got on stage, playing a song that you don't hear too much on TV (*Killing in the name* from Rage Against the Machine), Noel walked past her and she (who had plugs in her ears) spontaneously gave a fangirl cry that 'pierced his ears.'

Those who scored the most during the first part of the episode are – guess who – Lorenzo Licitra, Enrico Nigiotti and Måneskin. The tenor-crooner wins easily in his natural territory with *Who wants to live forever* by Queen and Nigiotti sings a song by the singer-songwriter Jovanotti, the one who went to school with Damiano's mother. Instead, Måneskin staged, in an acoustic set and with chains on Damiano's feet, *Flow* by Shawn James, he himself a former basketball player. Their performance is intense, so much so that Levante says: "I'm happy, for their performances always surprise me." Rita Bellanza had stated in her last video message that she felt her confidence renewed – yet she does not pass the first round.

As for the second round, contestants chose their own songs, yet it is still the exact same trio that fights for the podium. Andrea Radice, that sang in Italian for the first time during the first round, does not impress the judges and, by the end of the episode, he is out. Måneskin will come second, following *Million Reasons* by Licitra. Yet, their performance is hot and it's maybe one of the most remembered moments of *X-Factor Italy* since the beginning. Damiano, bare-legged in knee high stiletto boots, pole dances, whirling around. The lights are red. Then he rips off his fishnet top and stays bare-chested with duct tape on his nipples (yes, he did it before Vic) for the rest of the song. At the end, he raises a flap cut in his leather hot pants, showing a tattoo on his left buttock with the title of the Struts song he just sang: *Kiss this*. It's a taste of what Måneskin will do in the next four years. The official Facebook of *X-Factor Italy* defines the staging of the song as:

'The performance everyone is talking about.' The magazines elaborate on it immediately, they call Damiano: 'the fluid icon of the new sexuality.' Once out of the loft, he will reply: "I am not that fluid, I am very solid in fact. But I'm happy to have launched a trend: now we'll see men in heels and smoky eyes." In the same interview, Damiano confesses that *Kiss This* is the performance that cost him the most. During the *dailies*, he confessed that pole dancing: "is much more difficult than I thought, though it doesn't seem so." On the other hand, Manuel Agnelli commented:

> "If it works it is a coup worth trying. I can already imagine what they'll say after *Flow* [imitates the other judges] the tune is not energetic like the others, you work better on high-energy songs and so on and so on, and then BOOM! When it's time for *Kiss this* it'll be just like... ass in their faces!"

Luca Tommassini recalls the *Kiss this* episode in this way:

> "Damiano comes to me and says "I want to dance on heels and with my ass out." To support his request, he pulls down his pants and shows me a tattoo that reads 'Kiss this.' It was a risk, out of any TV standards, but the music was perfect and that performance has become one of the most beautiful flags of *X-Factor*: a manifesto of opportunities, a band that screamed for freedom."

Outside the loft, Rita Bellanza is interviewed by *Zoom Channel*. She speaks out about the judges and about Måneskin. With the rough honesty that distinguishes her (one of the various things of her that reminds you a young Ornella Vanoni) the singer shares her opinion about the band: "I believe that Måneskin are a force of nature. It's their characters I appreciate less, maybe. Damiano has a very strong character, perhaps he should soften it a little – but so do I." And so on:

"Damiano is a monster of talent onstage – *Kiss this*, come on... for me that's the top. I didn't see it at all like an arrogant gesture... he, oh well, is the top of arrogance, that is, if you want to be arrogant, go and take lessons from him and he will be able to teach you – I am not saying it's not useful. But that shouldn't become the only side you show of yourself, otherwise after a while "I am this... I am that... I am from Rome... where are you from?" hey... wait a minute... show the wonderful side that you have, because he has it. And yet on stage, he is ruthless and, in my opinion, he is fantastic for that. They are tough, they are very tough."

Then Rita makes a comparison with Ros saying that, if in her opinion they are stronger from a musical perspective, Måneskin have: "The look, they are very cool, Damiano has a voice that... wow! Ethan is very sweet, Er Cobra is always in my heart... that's it, they are cool. Well, I like them a lot"

Despite Rita's appreciation, as often happens, the media pumped up and misrepresented the bit about Damiano's arrogance. Rita's bluntness was not well rewarded and the singer had to make a video to rectify that: "the fact that Bellanza hates Måneskin is just bullshit." Damiano, at the end of the season, about Rita's remark on his arrogance, will say that: "it is a remark that finds little space in my thoughts, honestly. I don't consider myself arrogant... I actually consider myself very humble because I keep working a lot more than the others, so... it doesn't touch me."

In the video-diaries that followed live show number six, before the semifinal, Nigiotti admits he is getting thinner: "Maybe because I spend so much time with Måneskin, I regained the metabolism of a sixteen-year-old." He also speaks about a delicious two o'clock am pasta made by Thomas Er Cobbra with his little hands. Licitra also mentions food: his mother actually left Sicily to visit their loft to make sure that all the yummy food she sent was disposed of properly.

Måneskin obviously talk about the pole dance. "It was exhausting," says Damiano, "My legs are covered with bruises. Apart from that, it was truly a super-performance and – with all the modesty that defines us – we made history on *X-Factor*." And it's true in fact: no one had dared so much before. Once out of *X-Factor*, Damiano will remember his training as follows:

> "We started with a complete waxing, we did it together [points to Vic] ... so much fun. Then they called this teacher, a Ukrainian girl who made me do, something like nine hours a day, of that. Just that for five days. I did a tour de force. I walked around the loft wearing... that is, the stylists gave me high heeled shoes to learn to stand on them. As a final result, I was super-proud of what we all did together because in any case they too did a super-performance supporting such a shiny protagonist."

The band then announces the song of the next live show, *you're nobody till somebody loves you* by James Arthur, chosen by the public. James Arthur is one of Damiano's favorites, so he feels a certain responsibility on him.

On that very same day, that of the video-message, finally Damiano's brother, Vic's father, Ethan's mother, and Thomas's father went to the loft to visit them. A fan sent Thomas a t-shirt with "Er Cobra approves" written on it. Instead, Sandro De Angelis, Vic's father, brought a pair of funny underpants for the guitarist with a dangling cobra hanging from them.

Levante opens the seventh episode with a medley of her songs. On *Non me frega niente* (I do not care at all) all the contestants sing together – those who left the show, including: Rita, Sem&Stènn, Esposito, Camille and all the others are back on stage. The special guest is Francesca Michielin, we'll talk a lot about her throughout this story.

The contestants open the show by again singing their original songs that, after the fifth episode, are launched on the market. As they are stuck inside the loft and in the rehearsal room, they know little about how the songs are going. Some of them were able to catch some pieces of information from the radio, during the first time that all the contestants went on air at RTL, between the sixth and the seventh episode.

Then, in the second part of the show, Ros make their feature by staging a nineties Italian punk classic (*Acida* of Prozac +) yet their *Pretty Waste* by Bones that follows doesn't impress the judges. They go to the ballot with Samuel – the judges didn't like his *Feelin' Good* (Manuel Agnelli didn't like his *Stand by me* either). There's nothing left to do for Ros: the band tries *I Only Lie When I Love You* by Royal Blood – but fails. They're out. Yet, they are happy as they didn't expect to get to that point – the semifinals.

Måneskin are less convincing in staging *You're nobody till somebody loves you* than *Fais Le Mouv*. However, they reach the highest score of the evening, beating Licitra for a bit and taking the compliments of Mara Maionchi: "They communicate all right, he is definitely a first-class front-man." At the end of the evening, they are the only band left. The only contestants on Manuel Agnelli's team. Vic is the only woman.

And here we are: the last video-diaries, before the final show in the huge arena of the Assago Forum of Milan. All four (Licitra, Samuel Storm, Nigiotti, and Måneskin) are happy about having made it to the end. Before the last episode of *X-Factor* 2017, they took them to a wellness center to relax. Licitra explains that the show will be parted into three rounds: an international duet, a medley of three songs already staged during *X-Factor* live, and then everyone will perform their single. "We all won, in a way," says the tenor-crooner, "as there are four of us left." The special guest with whom the duet will be made is James Arthur, Damiano's idol. At the end of the video-diary, the band does not know what to say, so they play the game of silence – Damiano wins because Vic can't hold her laugh.

With James Arthur, Måneskin reach their highest score, Nigiotti follows. Oddly enough, Licitra does not impress the jury. However, he stays: it's Samuel Storm that has to leave the game. He places fourth. Both Fedez (men under twenty-five) and Levante (women under twenty-five) no longer have contestants in their teams.
Then it's medley time, Måneskin surprisingly enough, don't stage *Kiss this* but *Beggin'/ Take me out / Somebody told me*.

Ed Sheeran is the second special guest, after his bit, the host announces the finalists: despite his enormous progress remarked by Fedez, Nigiotti comes in third. Licitra and Måneskin then sing their original songs again: *In the name of love* and *Chosen*. Lorenzo Licitra wins by a 52.76% preference against Måneskin's 47.24%.

In the video that follows, Måneskin draw their conclusions: it happened all too fast, Vic has not yet rationalized that she was really part of the show, Er Cobbra feels he has improved on a technical level, Damiano as well. "Perhaps the only thing we don't feel now is fear," says Vic, "we feel we want to do new things." "Our dream now," adds Damiano, musing: "is a star on the Los Angeles Walk of Fame. We'll get there, we'll get there."
...and they really got to Los Angeles.

Of the other contestants, perhaps the one who made the best career is Enrico Nigiotti. He participated twice at the Sanremo Festival, and his ballad *Baciami adesso* (*Kiss Me Now*) was a radio hit. Rita Bellanza continues her career as a singer: she has recently been a guest on the tour of the singer-songwriter Marco Masini. Ros still play as a band; Camilla is also Bianca Atzei's guitarist (Atzei is a popular singer) and Samuel Storm has been the opening act to pop star Elodie. Lorenzo Licitra fluctuates between his crooner shows and some social events like *House of Gucci*'s premiere and the second wedding of Pavarotti's widow, Nicoletta Mantovani.

The tight rhythms of *X-Factor* have surely been excellent training for the future of each of them. After all, Samuel Storm said that the 'double speed' of life inside *X-Factor* would have turned helpful in the outside world. Luca

Tommassini remembers Måneskin as follows: "They were hungry for fame and life. Damiano told me: 'We want the world.' It was impossible to put the brakes on their talent."

Once out of X-Factor, Thomas got a huge cobra tattooed on his left arm.

Part 4.

2018-2020

*Måneskin are four cores that
form a single atom*
(Damiano)

B ack to the real world, Måneskin went through a long question-bombing session: journalists asked them everything they couldn't ask before. As for them, they were happy: "That's what we wanted, it is also a little more than what we wanted to be honest: we did not expect all this. So, we live it with positivity and smiles: deep down we are like children in a huge playground." Vic gives her favorite answer when asked how the group felt when they announced that the winner was Licitra: "E sticazzi!" ("fuck, yeah!") In early December, *Chosen* is awarded a gold record. Damiano dedicated it to all the professionals without whom *X-Factor* wouldn't be possible:

"To the whole, massive machine that works in the background: to the editorial office – those guys are in a certain way like our guardian angels in there, they are the ones who stayed with us 24 hours a day; to the production guys the ones who provide us all the materials we needed; to the toolmakers, to Luca [Tommassini], to the producers, to the other contestants, to the make-up artists ["to the make-up artists that make us look cool" adds Vic], to the hairdressers, to the costume designers, to all those who have made all this possible."

They often mentioned Luca Tommassini's name. A reporter from *Ginger Generation* asks what it was like working with him. Vic points out that:

"We collaborated with him and he gave us the opportunity to put all our ideas on stage, we collaborated with him and we created things together. Yet, basically, everything we did is also our idea. We got there together."

"The pole was our idea," Damiano claims, "*Kiss This* was the most we could dare. We did it more for us than for the audience." As for makeup and costumes, Damiano adds:

"I feel lucky because I have my stage persona but the stage persona I bring is 100% me, I never fake it. About the fluid thing... guys, I am not fluid at all, I'm steady on my side. I like to wear make-up, I like to act over the top, I like to have fun then... concerning that aspect, I'm like Nigiotti."

One question inevitably is about fashion: how did you choose your clothes before arriving here? "As I said before, we are normal kids," replies Damiano, yet the journalist doesn't buy it: "It's hard to believe!" The front-man continues:

"We lived by allowances or by the money we collected by playing on the street, so it was all about second-hand markets... things stolen from my grandmother, things stolen from my grandfather... My grandfather has style... so we wore what we had, keeping our very specific taste."

Måneskin feel the support of family and friends: Damiano says that his brother Jacopo and his best friend ran the band's Facebook profile when they were inside *X-Factor*, Vic had left her page to two of her friends, Ethan had his sisters managing his page and Thomas had his father. "My parents have seen me failing everything in life," admits Damiano talking to *Il Corriere della Sera*, "And then they saw me giving a hundred percent on this one." It came naturally for them to support him.

On Licitra, Damiano says: "He is a great singer and inside *X-Factor* he learned to become a performer as well. To his credit, he is amazing, Lorenzo is amazing, he is tough." On the fact that Italian major labels do not love rock very much, the audience of mainstream music is not used to it, Vic adds: "And then, this was *X-Factor Italy*. If they do *X-Factor International* maybe we might win it."

Speaking of Galassi's prediction, on the fact that the music market would inevitably try to split Damiano from the rest of the band, the front-man himself states in a press conference, (showing cast-iron ethics, behind his *coatto*-attitude):

"To be honest, this group already existed before I arrived, they took me in, not otherwise. Ok, then they accepted my leadership, but I'm not a supervisor, I'm not a boss. I am a leader, I am part of the band, I am not ahead of them. Instead, sometimes I am behind them, to push them. So, any offer that might come to me would not make me quit them because I was absolutely nothing before I met them. I mean, although I may still be nothing now, I am at least a grain of sand: before them, I did not exist either as a singer or even as an idea of a singer. Hence, this is a non-problem because I can't see a future for me without them, ever."

"Otherwise, they would be the Damiano David band, but I don't want that" he adds, interviewed by *Rumors.it*.

In December, Damiano already knows that he will not go back to school. Er Cobbra instead intends to finish the two years left, both Vic and Ethan will finish their studies through homeschooling. Outside *X-Factor*, Vic declares that she wants to go shopping as soon as possible, but Damiano – that actually has got a little chip on his shoulder – declares: "I'm going to school to do this... [obscene gesture]"

"There's one thing that the whole of Italy wants to know," a journalist asks Vic and Damiano, "are you together or not?" "No" they answer, then they add simultaneously: "We are not engaged, we are engaging." Betta Carbone, one of the interviewers, then asks Damiano: "Do you know that you are a dream for women, even some over-forties?" and he goes: "I'm open to everything: over, under. I'm single, so..."

Yet, it must have been more or less in that period that Damiano met his partner, Giorgia Soleri, since, after Sanremo, in one of the very few references to his private life, the singer wrote on Instagram: "After almost four years we can say it – can't we?" over one of their rare couple photos.

But Betta Carbone, posing that question, was referring to a bizarre phenomenon dubbed "Mammeskin" (Momeskin), which is a middle-aged fan group that gathered on a

Facebook page, who describes itself as a: "Fan page for those who are no longer little girls, and by date of birth, could be their mothers.". Mammeskin appreciate all the four members of the group – Damiano above all. They launched such a trend that even in an article of the *Corriere della Sera*, by the end of the year, the journalist Paolo Giordano speaks of Måneskin's: "Explosive sex appeal, which has turned troops of mothers – with children the same age as the band – into teenagers out of control." According to Giordano himself, jokes aside, after *X-Factor* Måneskin have made on many: "The effect of an awakening. It doesn't happen frequently. In fact, it seldom happens."

In early December, the band had shot the second video of *Chosen*, the only one now available. In the concept of the video, there are all the fantasies they put on stage during those months, including pole dancing "We just have to be ourselves," said Damiano while recording it, "besides, the level of photography, direction, and production is so high that it's light-years above what we could afford, so... it's a great experience." Once out of the TV show, he will add:

"They took us to this hotel, there was the track for the camera and we had to rehearse every scene, beginning to end, before we could act them in a row. And it was exhausting because the whole sequence is so full of things, that is, in four rooms, a hundred things happen in each scene, a thousand changes of clothes... we shot for fifteen to sixteen hours, it was very tough. But eventually, we saw the final result and it was... wow!"

And so on:

"It was fun that scene in which there are, like, insiders, directors, thirty extras, and me naked in this corridor... I think you noticed that we have this slight tendency to excess and that we are comfortable when things are over the top, so in all honestly, being naked is not a big deal for me."

On *Chosen*, Damiano had declared at the *X-Factor* press conference:

"I write in Italian as well. This is the original song we brought to the auditions and it is our first official song so we wanted it to be sponsored by this massive machine that is *X-Factor*. Still, in the pipeline, we have many tunes in Italian and English. It'd be cool to write in French, Spanish, or Turkish. But, yeah, we also write in Italian. Mainly in Italian lately."

"One can always go further," then declares the front-man, "but we are lucky enough to have a lifetime to go further. We have no regrets whatsoever."
The band is already in a frame of mind to take this as a job.

The *Chosen* EP was released on December 8, while the band was still on the show. The production is handled, once again, by the best professional that Måneskin – as beginners – could get: Lucio Fabbri. Fabbri lived through the Milanese scene of the seventies until he joined the PFM band as a violinist in 1979. From the nineties onwards, he has been one of the most requested rock-pop producers on the market. In 2011, he performed live with Dan Aykroyd and Jim Belushi, as part of the Blues Brothers Band. Måneskin were lucky enough to find him on their way, as at the time he was the musical director of *X-Factor*, and has been for thirteen seasons. In addition to 'the title track', the *Chosen* EP contains the other original song that was ready (*Recovery*), and some covers performed at *X-Factor* (*Beggin', Let's Get It Started, Somebody Told Me, You need me, I don't need you, Io vengo dalla luna*). The band directly produced the two songs written by them, leaving the covers to Fabbri. A month later, the EP was certified Platinum; in April it will go Platinum twice.

It will climb back into the charts – the international charts this time – In 2021.

The band then signs for Sony Music, the manager who selects the interviews and TV appearances for them is Marta Donà, who already has Marco Mengoni, the winner of *X-Factor* 2009, in her roster. A few days after the end of the TV show, on December 20, 2017, the dates of the first important Måneskin tour and of the autograph signings of CDs and LPs in bookstores, that will take place in January, are released. In four hours, the gigs in Parma, Genoa, Bologna, Naples, Palermo, and of course Rome are sold out. The signings are very crowded. Damiano will say to the magazine *Sorrisi e Canzoni*:

"After the final episode [of *X-Factor*], you get out of a world that was totally different from the real world – you forget what the real world is like. We found ourselves overwhelmed by everything that is happening now, which is beautiful, but we need time to become conscious of it."

In that same interview, Thomas is amazed that their audience is intergenerational. Damiano adds:

"Yesterday something beautiful happened: we took a picture with a fifty-year-old mother, her twenty-year-old daughter and her other daughter of seven: three generations, all with us. I thought about it for a moment, and I told myself: what a fuckin 'pleasure!'"

The new year is 2018.

Måneskin start it out with their first appearance on the most important public network, Rai 1. It is January 7, 2018, the day before Damiano's nineteenth birthday. The TV show is *Che tempo che fa* (*What's the weather like*) – which is not a weather forecast television program, but a classic talk show hosted by Fabio Fazio, the format is his idea. Carlo Verdone, previously interviewed on his new film, introduces them. We've mentioned him before: he is the comedian and author/director/main actor from the film *Gallo Cedrone* (among many others) about the typical *coatto* of Rome. The four Måneskin members obviously love him, "How cool is that!" Says Damiano, happy that Verdone likes them, "You're great Carlo, you're number one!" The band plays *Chosen* live. The due interview follows but Verdone can't hold himself back and intervenes, telling Thomas that a certain thing he did on the guitar reminded him of *Wanton Song* by Led Zeppelin and "it was fantastic." Verdone looks very moved. It's known that he is a great rock fan (he is also famous for having made David Bowie angry just by mentioning David Sylvian). "There is something in there," his words, "gorgeous sound, amazing voice... they are very good: I foresee an outstanding future." The comedian looks as happy as a child when someone plays rock and roll.

On the other hand, Fazio is amazed by how the four kids act maturely – one of them is almost nineteen, all the others were still underage. So, he asks them if they have always been like this. "Yes, actually," replies Damiano, "the only difference is that now we have more means to do what we want to do, but all this has always been our first idea and we used to stage it how we could. Now we are lucky to have all the resources we need: all the gigs are already sold out: Milan, Turin... this way we can express ourselves one hundred percent."

At that point, they discover that the *Chosen* LP went Platinum, it is Fazio that gives it to them.

The host of *X-Factor Italia;* Alessandro Cattelan, at the time, had a talk show on Sky One called *And then there is Cattelan* (*E dopo c'è Cattelan*). Måneskin were his guests by the end of January, they hadn't seen him for a month. During the show, he insists on their youth, asking them if they still live with their parents – well, yes – and, what their parents' advice is before they go on tour or to the signings: "They tell me to, 'cover yourself up!'" says Damiano.

On the arrogance of their stage personas, Cattelan says: "I had the pleasure of meeting these guys: they are super cute, they are super nice, but the first time we saw them at *X-Factor* during the auditions, I remember that everyone wanted to punch you, as at first glance you have these ...straight faces" "...asshole faces," concludes Damiano adding that, in his opinion, "changing people's minds," that is, entering the program as assholes and leaving as nice guys, has been among some of the fun things from *X-Factor*.

On the show, the band also talks about the first VIP followers on Instagram they had, their IG channel had almost 400,000 followers at the time including the showgirl Belen Rodriguez, and James Arthur ("Damiano's idol, who follows me and me only" says Vic). Thomas mentions the TV commentator Alba Parietti, TV host Alessia Marcuzzi and, of course, Carlo

Verdone. All super-known characters in Italy, I wrote a tiny dictionary for you at the bottom of this book if you get lost. Alessia Marcuzzi (former *Big Brother* host) has a passion for fashion and style, that's why she followed Victoria with a certain interest. "Yes, she does," says the bass player, "she sent me like a picture and the caption was 'I'm just like you,' and I wrote to her in reply: 'Do you know how many sub-brand cereals you gotta eat to be like me...!?'" *Coatto* attitude strikes again, Marcuzzi just laughed in response. Then Cattelan shows them pictures of some famous people who characterized his generation (like Mahoney from Police Academy and football player Paul "Gazza" Gascoigne). It's kind of creepy how the band only recognizes Margaret Thatcher, that's part of history, among all the other pop references of Y generation: actors, soccer players and singers meant nothing to them. Young people, *indeed* they are. The interview ends with a story about Ethan and his being the *quiet one* (in this phase of Måneskin, he seldom spoke). Cattelan tells the audience that during the final live show of *X-Factor*:

> "After one of their performances, there was Ethan who was playing the drums suspended in the air above the Assago Forum. We go down, the audience had to vote so they all come to me but one was missing. I turn my head, and since he never speaks, we didn't realize he [Ethan] was still standing on top of the platform, that was tilted."

...and the poor thing made some shy gestures to be noticed. It was the same stage that tested Damiano's vertigo.

At the beginning of 2018 interviews flourished: on Rosario Fiorello's radio show (we will meet him again in Sanremo), for the magazine *Glamour*, for the opening of a Condé Nast event, during the crazy signing in the Amazon offices in Milan – playing with water pistols. Then the gigs: the winter tour is completely sold-out, so other dates come out concerning the fall. Manuel Agnelli then wants them as guests on *Ossigeno*, and Måneskin really can't say no to him. It is March 8.

On March 23, *Morirò da re* (*I will die like a king*), the following single, in Italian, is released. It anticipates the band's first album, *Il ballo della vita* (*The dance of life*). In a funny video, in which Ethan, with his characteristic aplomb translates the words of the others speaking in the dialect of Rome, Måneskin announce some prizes for those who will listen to their new single more than others on the Sony website. Their official Facebook page describes the new song as follows: "It is a tune that speaks out, or shall we say, gives answers. It gives answers to your doubts and represents our work. It is a song that shows that music is always at the center of everything and rumors count for nothing." Two days later, *Morirò da re* is already on top of the iTunes charts.

Måneskin present their song on TV once again at Fabio Fazio's, *Che tempo che fa*. When Fazio asks if the video, which is due to come out the next day, "is not over-the-top" Damiano replies "Of course not!" Of course...

The teaser video is not over the top, all right: fast-forward fifty seconds to Damiano's long make-up session that turns him into a drag-ish woman. The video itself is very simple: Måneskin's caravan, Ethan bare-chested with a snake on his shoulders, and Damiano also bare-chested – but that's not new – wearing a corset. Also, simple and not over the top at all is the glamorous circus of the second part of the video, the cyberpunk automaton. Er Cobbra, with his face all blue and glittery (because, like a good snake, he sheds his skin) and Victoria with dark-angel wings. Ethan has *many* snakes on him now, and Damiano... well, he is unrecognizable and more ambiguous than ever. The concept of the video may remind you of a movie from some years later, *Freaks Out* by Gabriele Mainetti (he himself also from Rome), where the protagonists are a gang of "circus-X Men" during the war. "A wonderful happy world, that of the freaks," says Damiano while backstage. A perfect set for this sensual, extreme, and proud love song that soon becomes a radio hit. Meanwhile, on April 20, the red vinyl of the *Chosen* EP is out. In the same month, with a picture, the band announces that they are back in Rome – 'as kings.' In the picture they are wearing Mac Cosmetics make-up, the hairdo is by Tony & Guy and it looks like Victoria came out of the manga *Lamù* by Rumiko Takahashi from the way she dresses.

Meanwhile, the gigs in Milan triple and they double in Florence. Tickets sell like hotcakes. In between trains, for they travelled by train, the band posts funny short videos, like the one where Vic and Thomas listen to some music of dubious taste, going wild while Ethan sleeps. One month after the release of *Morirò da re*, the studio session video is launched. The Italian version of SNL is not as important and legendary as the US one, there is even a host – the comedian Claudio Bisio – who was however, the soul of similar TV shows in the past. Måneskin are his guests in April 2018. On May 7, *Morirò da re* is certificated gold, a month later the band plays at the Wind Music Awards inside the stunning Arena of Verona. After that, there is a gig for Radio Italia in front of the Milan Cathedral. In the summer, *Morirò da re* goes platinum. On the official Facebook page, Måneskin post a picture taken in via del Corso taken exactly one year before, the caption goes: "Last summer we played in small clubs in Rome, while this summer…" That summer, the summer of 2018, everything changed.

The four are the new testimonials for the advertising of a well-known brand of chewing gum, and from there, we have their first big international tour: Hamburg, Santiago de Compostela, and back to *Milan Rocks,* where Måneskin will be Imagine Dragons' opening act. The gigs for fall 2018 are all sold out. "We don't forget when there was no one in front of our stage," they write on the official Facebook page, "Today we are sold-out everywhere." On social media, they often joke on those who, in the past, had called them a 'temporary phenomenon' ("Thinking back to when they told us that we wouldn't have lasted more than three months").

The new recording session is due to start in May – the new album is scheduled for October. There is time, in September, to go back to *X-Factor* – as guests. The band performs the new single, *Torna a casa (Come back home)*, on TV: it is a ballad where the character of Marlena reappears. In the previous tune, that was the lover close to whom Damiano would have died like a king, instead here, he loses her as one can lose a muse. Marlena almost seems like a poignant and desperate metaphor of music, of coming back home and to one's self after six crazy months and a year out of the ordinary. "Marlena is like Venus for the band," they explain, "the personification of our freedom, creativity, and life." It almost looks like another *Marlena* – the tragic and transgressive character from Julie Buntin's debut novel. *Torna a casa* is yet something else the audience doesn't expect from Måneskin. An introspective, raw ballad. Another smash.

This time the video is actually rather simple – apart from the location, the splendid Villa Arconati in Bollate near Milan, called "the little Versailles," the main character is a dancer – pale and on crutches – who comes back to dance while the guys play.

Il ballo della vita (The dance of life), a title that everyone knows, were it not for Damiano's tattoo on his chest, comes out right after *Torna a casa*'s release, on October 3, 2018, exactly one year after *X-Factor* 2017. On Facebook, Måneskin present the record as follows:

> "Finally, here we are, we are really back.
> We come back to give you joy, happiness, tears, and euphoria. To give you life.
> And it is *Il ballo della vita*, it is the exaltation of our youth, of our passion.
> It's the love that runs red in our veins and which hopefully will reach your heart.
> It's the dance of life my love, let's dance."

Later, Vic will say:

> "The title we chose for our first record fully represents the concept of it: dancing is an act that brings people together, that sets them free, that makes them lose all the superstructures to let out the most spontaneous part of us. And that's what we tried to achieve with this record."

In the advertising launch, Måneskin deliberately choose to use some of the 'best' insults of social media haters, to disempower them and to raise awareness against cyberbullying. "If someone insults you, it is because you are good," said Damiano when interviewed on the radio show *Radio Two Social Club*.

At the same time, an event film about the making of the disc, *This is Måneskin*, is screened at the cinema. During the premiere at home in Rome, a gig precedes the film.

The four Måneskin members wrote *Il ballo della vita* in a villa outside Milan, in Garlasco. An actual villa, with a swimming pool, a rehearsing room with instruments, four bedrooms, and a TV for Er Cobbras PlayStation, which he had brought from home. That villa is actually L'Angelo Studio, the recording studio of singer-songwriter Ron, that loaned it to Måneskin for the occasion. It was Fabrizio Ferraguzzo's idea – he was Måneskin's producer then. There they spent about a month (May-June 2018).

In the film, Ethan stands out a little more than usual (at the time he was noticeably quiet if compared to the other three), we finally notice his slight not-rolling 'r' and his ability to calm spirits down. Thomas, that summer, has his driving license exam (which goes wrong), in addition to school, where he has to take a test to access the fifth year of Liceo Scientifico. Poor Ethan helps him, like an older brother, by listening to what the guitarist had learned about chemical bonds, sine and cosine. Actually, his exam (this is not on film, Thomas tells *Radio Due Social Club* the whole story a month later) was on the day after the gig at the Arena of Verona during the Wind Music Award. "I had to wake up at half-past four in the morning. So, on one hour of sleep, I went there to take my exam and I passed it!" Ethan and Vic also have school, we see them studying sometimes.

Over the course of the film, Er Cobbra thinks a lot about the band, how much he wanted to be in a band before Måneskin, and how it comes across that band dynamics force its members to discuss their ideas with others. Being part of a group is a recurring theme of the film, the discipline and professional maturity of the four is stunning. They fight, but this does not undermine their project: discussions are occasions to stand up for an idea in a constructive confrontation since everything must be approved by four heads. Vic stands out as a strong yet impulsive character. It is remarkably interesting what she says about having to manage the band as a big thing, 'as adults,' as the main cause of internal quarrels. After all, Måneskin were four guys not even in their twenties who, at that point, couldn't make mistakes.

Thomas stands out as the music monomaniac, devoted to rock, so much so that he gets angry when he has the slightest suspicion that the others turned into yes wo/men to please Ferraguzzo, dismissing his ideas. Ethan, on the other hand, is silent but indispensable: he makes others think, he makes some order in the rehearsal room and in his friends' heads when they get angry. Damiano, the eldest, wonders if his older-brother attitude sometimes turns into an asshole attitude – at times, he proves to be incredibly stressed, very tired. For instance, when he confesses to Vic that he was so nervous he was afraid he wouldn't make it to the end of the winter tour. The singer is definitely the most pressure-conscious and encourages others to be aware of what they have become. According to Damiano, they don't have to believe the narrative that wants to show them as 'fucking child prodigies': they are musicians and, in spite of their strengths and weaknesses, they aim high.

That's how they wrote and recorded *Il ballo della vita*. The band celebrates their achievement, coming back to Rome and resting for a while. No double-speed rhythms. Through soccer, bowling... those things that all teenagers do, Måneskin allow themselves the luxury of pretending to live like all their peers.

Besides *Morirò da re* and *Torna a casa* (that *Rockol* defined as: "The most well-crafted and mature song on the record"), in *Il ballo della vita* Thomas's funk-rock imprint comes out in songs like *New Song* and *Fear for Nobody*. In *Sh * t Blvd* it blends well with Damiano's taste for soul and reggaeton, so much so that *All Music Italy* dares to say that these two songs might work abroad, beyond the Alps. In *Lasciami Stare* (*Leave me alone*), Thomas and Vic show their love for the Red Hot Chili Peppers. *L'altra dimensione* (*The other dimension*) is a song for dancing where the muse Marlena appears in the chorus and where you can sense a subtle influence of the tune that Nigiotti always sang at *X-Factor*, *Il mio nemico* by Daniele Silvestri ("they sell their love through with Visa cards"). In *Le parole lontane* (*Distant words*) – a ballad that came out of a riff from Thomas during an improvisation – Damiano projects his anxiety towards the future. It looks like the song is about a relationship that falls apart, or is it? Maybe it's rather the fear of losing Marlena that the lyrics express – that is, the connection with music, with the freedom to be oneself, with magic. On the track list, this classic ballad comes before *Immortale* feat. Vegas Jones, a curious choice. We spoke about Vegas Jones, whose genre is trap music, when Måneskin covered his song *Trankilo*. *Immortale* follows the self-celebration trend of hip hop while the vocal details in the background belong to the Puerto-Rican-Italian trap genre. Damiano here sings with autotune. Later, he'll speak about this incursion into trap music:

"We chose to do this featuring because we are children of this generation, and we are also influenced by this kind of music, that we like. In this record, we wanted to put all our influences, and my writing takes also from the metric of trap and hip hop. We wanted to show that a band can write and play that genre."

In *Are you ready?* instead, the most danceable side of Damiano comes out, as he sings in ragamuffin style. On the track list, *Close to the top* follows, it's a classic rock piece with old-school echoes from the seventies including a grand finale with a voice and guitar duet like Bowie's *Suffragette City*. We might say that in this first record, Måneskin can't help out-of-rock digressions. The tune that follows is *Niente da dire* (*Nothing to say*). Ethan there plays on pads and Damiano struggles with lines and Italian accents. Here as well, we can notice Daniele Silvestri's influences. After all, Damiano's first memory related to music is one of his songs.

Rockol magazine's reviewer doesn't tolerate ambiguities: it's either Italian or English, pop-rock or something else, new sound or old school. And yet, the vastness of the musical (and linguistic) references of *Il ballo della vita* is one of its points of strength. An actual fluid identity – artistically-wise – still today represents one of the key features of the band: Måneskin search for the music they would like to listen to, they don't wish to confine themselves under labels, under constraining definitions.

Not surprisingly, Sony had given them the power to do whatever they wanted. The key to the whole record is perhaps hidden in *L'altra dimensione (The other Dimension)* – the title of the album, by the way, is taken from its chorus. Like Manuel Agnelli before them, the four Måneskin members have chosen music to stay far away from a dull world that has already left scars on them. The world they want to be part of is pink, creative, and open. The video of the song underlines this aspect.

As for Marlena, Damiano defines her on *Vanity Fair* as: "Freedom of expression. It is an invitation to express yourself, to be creative, to find your potential and to improve yourself." If this is the muse, to keep narrow boundaries would have been a contradiction. And after all, the Beatles mixed genres – didn't they? A record like *The White Album* is made of Sitar songs, tape-loop experiments, classic ballads, rock and roll, vaudeville-style pieces, etc.

On that same *Rockol* review, however, as early as October 2018, it's written that Licitra almost disappeared at a mainstream level.

Now it's time for a bookshop tour to sign records, all the events are as crowded as ever. *Torna a casa* turns gold in two weeks, it goes platinum in one month. *Il ballo della vita* also certifies golden in one week, platinum in one month. In November, Måneskin's international tour starts. The gigs are in Spain, Germany, Belgium, Switzerland, and France. The grand finale is in London. Meanwhile, the Italian tour doubles its dates. The band is now Diesel's testimonial, they take self-ironic pictures of them holding denim jackets with 'soon to be forgotten' written on them.

The showman Fiorello calls them to appear again on his radio program, where the band has fun covering the theme song of one of the most popular anime cartoons on Italian TV based on soccer, *Captain Tsubasa* (*Holly and Benji*). Damiano changes the name of the main character, 'Holly' the goal-scorer, to 'Totti', a former captain and one of the symbols of his football team – Roma. Vevo then patronizes an unplugged session, Måneskin release a very intense version of *Torna a casa* and *Morirò da re. Vanity Fair Italy* interviews them, Damiano already has the album title tattooed on his chest and, when the journalist remarks that it's like getting a girlfriend's name tattooed, he replies: "Not at all, for me this record is like a son and you love a son forever."

It turns out that the band – especially the front-man – already has a certain hardcore fan base that leaves them explicit sexual messages. Some *Mammeskin* often try to touch the backside of the singer when they have the chance. In the same interview, the Capricorn side of Damiano also emerges: he is disciplined and self-regulating and he has the tendency to impose his rules on others out of 'respect for the public.' No drugs and no junk food allowed on tour. So much so that Vic confesses that once she hid in her room to eat chips.

That of Damiano's strict rules, a topic that also comes up on the radio show *Radio Due Social Club* hosted by songwriter and radio speaker Luca Barbarossa, and comedian Andrea Perroni. Damiano's mother Rossella loves the show while Barbarossa's little daughter is in the studio because she loves Måneskin, to the point that when she met them, she exclaimed: "I forgot how to breathe." The four speak of divergences in cooking pasta (Ethan's is too underdone though he calls it *al dente*), of Ethan's famous hen: 'Highlander,' who unfortunately died from a fatal encounter with a fox and, finally, of differences in musical tastes. "In the van, we have a rule," says Damiano, "each of us is entitled to put a song on when our turns come and that song is unquestionable – otherwise we fight."

"I like putting on instrumental pieces from the seventies up to eight minutes long," says the drummer.

"And we like very much listening to them, insulting him" concludes the singer.

When Barbarossa tells Damiano that, given the lyrics he writes, he took: "good revenge on your literature teacher," the front-man confesses that some other teacher wrote to him saying that she was using the lyrics of *Torna a casa* to explain the Dolce Stil Novo to her pupils ("And they flunked me for Italian literature!"). In fact, Marlena looks a little like the muses of Dante and Petrarch: Beatrice and Laura were not just women but symbols of art and life.

The two hosts then challenge Måneskin to identify songs: Damiano is strong on Italian repertoire, Vic on classic rock, and Ethan on prog-rock. All of them fail on the Italian pop from the sixties, on a band called the Camaleonti. Meanwhile, a Facebook user writes under the radio show video podcast: "You have raised the level of *X- Factor* so much that this year the show is a total disappointment." (Actually, rapper Anastasio and Leo Gassmann, grandson of the famous actor Vittorio, both from that season, will have brilliant careers).

Meanwhile, *Torna a casa* became the closing theme of the Netflix TV series *Baby*.

Like a reality TV show, the Måneskin tour is filmed and cut into short promotional clips. In those videos, the band is followed in between concerts; in swimming pools, in make-up sessions, during rehearsals, when unwanted exchanges of clothes happen before going onstage, when Damiano stage-dives, when Ethan teaches how to pretend to drink alcohol to be credible at a party, when Ethan juggles, when Vic eats chips and has anxious dreams, when Thomas makes fun of Ethan's "r" saying "touv Euvopeo," when Vic and Thomas do rap challenges, when the fans are screaming, and onstage. In

December 2018, the new gigs for the following year are also sold out.

Måneskin start 2019 from Sardinia, doing a gig in Olbia. In early January, *Torna a casa* goes platinum. The gigs in Lugano and London are soon sold out, the gig in Hamburg is to be moved to a larger venue, the London gig has to be doubled. They announced this last news on Facebook, the caption goes: "How do you say *'presto dimenticati'* in English?" (Soon forgotten)

"Guys, you know what I was thinking," Ethan says in *Il ballo della vita TOUR* episode two, "this kind of life is just beautiful."

The new single released is *Fear for Nobody*, the video follows shortly after. It's all based on rewind used as a choreographic effect. It's January 18, 2019, Thomas's birthday. On that day, all four Måneskin members are officially no longer underage. For the third time, the band comes back to Fabio Fazio's *Che tempo che fa* to perform their new single and *Torna a casa*. "You don't sound like anything else and that's really good," says the host who then jokes on the fact that Vic played *Smoke on the Water* in that famous video when she was eight, yet she ignores the most famous Italian children's songs like *La sveglia birichina*. Meanwhile, the summer tour is all sold out.

For the first time, the most important news program on public network TV (Tg1) is interested in Måneskin: Damiano and Thomas give a taste of *Fear for Nobody*, guitar and vocals only. The rhythm section dances. Then the veteran journalist Vincenzo Mollica interviews them. "Beyond all the successes – the platinum discs, the streaming rates – the four of us are what matters the most," says Damiano, "our dream is to wake up every morning and have a new goal to achieve. That is, if we get to play at Wembley, then we want to do... Wembley part two." "We want to avoid settling for what we achieved, we want to get higher and higher," adds Victoria, "also musically-wise, we want to keep improving ourselves more and more."

At Eurovision, to the microphones of *Eurovoxx*, Damiano will say that this living 'day by day' is what "helps us to be really grounded and professional."

The tour goes on. Måneskin launch a compilation on Spotify that includes the famous van songs, one from each of them. Meanwhile, Fabio Fazio keeps supporting and following the band. He sends them one of his best associates, the melodic singer Orietta Berti (born in 1943). In February 2019 Orietta Berti, who looks like a good-natured seemingly innocent grandmother, reaches Måneskin's van leaving for Zurich. On the way, she has a chat with them: she makes sure that Thomas is of age, she compliments Ethan for his beauty and for the way he plays, she takes makeup lessons from Vic then she gives advice to Damiano for keeping his throat healthy. Orietta is well-known for her beautiful crystalline voice – her advice though is a bit hardcore: in her opinion, the front-man should eat red chilies an hour before getting onstage.

Backstage in Zurich, Orietta and Damiano sing *Morirò da re* together.

Meanwhile, *L'altra dimensione* is the new single and it goes gold immediately. Its video, set in a kind of multi-ethnic and multicolored court of miracles, follows. *Cosmopolitan Italy* dedicates the cover of the magazine to Måneskin: the title goes: *Sex, drugs? We prefer discipline. Cosmo* confronts Damiano on the arrogance thing that has emerged for the first time since Rita Bellanza's exit from *X-Factor* and later became a constant background buzz behind Måneskin. The singer replies as follows:

"If I didn't believe in myself, if I wasn't a little vain, how could I do this job? On stage, it's okay to rock it all. It is in everyday life that you have to be humble: with the people who work with you, for example, and in making music. If there is to rehearse and play, we never back down. And we follow very strict rules."

Years earlier, Vic had said in this regard that:

"In my opinion, self-confidence and arrogance should not be confused, because self-confidence in my opinion, is a very important value. Everyone should be confident because, in the end, you have to be yourself all your life, so you have to be happy with who you are. And if you are not sure of yourself, it is also very difficult, perhaps, doing this profession, going on stage, showing millions of people your work, what you are, what you want to say."

Måneskin fans know by now that statements like "we'll take it all," are typical of the band, more than arrogance, it represents a (fair) gut reaction to a world wary of young creatives and of creativity itself. Måneskin confidently affirm that they have chosen to challenge this mistrust, they have chosen to be aware of the fact that success comes from hard work. That's what makes them so fascinating. Damiano keeps talking, and it's a slap in the face to all those who believe in innate talent, that is, that either you're born Mozart or it's not worth it:

"I'm full of flaws, I came out wrong, I was terrible at school, I don't come from a good family. I'm a common guy struggling, like anyone. Yet, I followed my aspirations and somehow, I made it. In short, you don't need to be perfect to succeed. All you need to do is work your ass off."

A particularly important singer-songwriter who fought so much against this mistrust of creativity, Luigi Tenco, said: "I also believe that a man should be entirely what he wants to be. The important thing is to know what you want. And I think I know. Is it this self-confidence that bothers so many people?" It is a phrase that also fits Måneskin a lot.

In that same interview for *Cosmo,* Damiano's very strict rules are back:

"When we're on tour, it's okay to have fun, but we must keep a high level of performance on stage, we must think straight and keep the mind cool to do the right things, technically-wise. So, zero fast food, you don't eat shit. Coke and fizzy drinks are ok, but not too much. Alcohol, a little. You don't come back at four in the morning, there's no need."

Perhaps Vic De Angelis is the only bassist in the history of rock and roll to have a "chip dealer." But Damiano is firm:

"I am a former basketball player, my discipline comes from there, and, yes, I am the one who sets the rules, the ball-buster. I am very strict with myself, and if I want others to do as I do, I have to set a good example. Then I am the oldest and, as I've lived a little more than them, maybe I see responsibilities first."

Måneskin is not Guns N' Roses, that's for sure. This interview makes all the Eurovision fuss sound like nonsense. Damiano keeps talking – and he seems to have rationalized and elaborated all the self-destruction of almost eighty years of rock and roll:

"Anyone can do "sex & drugs." It's certainly not what makes you cool. Being an artist is a great thing. Creating art, writing songs... Noticing how people look at us when we are on stage: that's awesome. The cool part of it is not when a picture of me comes out and I look good and I'm with some women. I mean, this is also cool. But after ten minutes the feeling has already passed."

And more:

"We have always been told that we are lazy, that we don't want to achieve anything in life. But I see many guys who are committed to something. Of course, we were lucky, we were born with this path straight ahead and our psychology, it made things easier for us. What we want to do is to put this gift of ours at the service of others. By making music and saying that everyone has the freedom to be who they are."

The front-man also speaks about women:

"Yes, I was always lucky on that side. Now... they're like war machines. They throw bras at us like they did to Vasco Rossi. He was the last one they threw bras at, wasn't he?

Then mothers arrive at the signing of our records with their children, sometimes small ones, and sometimes it happens that while Vic is taking care of the kids, the mothers tell me: "Can I give you a kiss, can I touch your ass?""

Check the tiny dictionary at the end of this book to see who Vasco Rossi is. We'll mention him again, later.

It's the spring of 2019, the Måneskin tour goes on. In April, all four get the letters "Må" tattooed on themselves in London, this seals the band's synergy once and for all. For Ethan and Vic, it is their first tattoo. The backstage series *Il ballo della vita tour* now includes half an hour of film concerning the European gigs: Barcelona, Zurich, Hamburg, London, Munich, and Lugano. The band shops in vintage stores, Vic skates, Er Cobbra either plays guitar or plays games on his PlayStation (but then he shows concerns towards Ethan, who doesn't eat enough, like a brother), Damiano goes wild on stage.

In May *Le parole lontane* turns gold, it goes platinum in September. The video is released on September 13, with sepia-toned cinematography and a slight Bertolucci's *The Dreamers* atmosphere. The four Måneskin members flirt with Marlena in a farmhouse close to an industrial ruin, but then Marlena vanishes.

In summer, the band is awarded at the SEAT Music Awards (former Wind Music Awards). Then they play at Aperol Happy Together Live in Piazza San Marco in Venice, hosted once again by Alessandro Cattelan with Francesca Michielin. In June, a year has passed since the production of *Il ballo della vita*. In November, the gig at the Dome, in London, gets sold out.

In short, this was 2019 for Måneskin: a series of gigs, backstage videos, traveling around Italy, abroad, and back again.

2020

On January 5, 2020, under a video of backstage from the tour, on the official Facebook page of Måneskin, the caption is: "You do not know what's coming." Unfortunately, in this case, it was them – like the rest of the world – who didn't know what 2020 would have in store.

There are no posts until March 10, 2020. In Italy, that was the second day of the first lockdown. Måneskin's post says:

"We are passing through hard times, many of us are scared, it is understandable. The desire to go outside, to meet each other, to share interests, to touch each other; the desire to laugh together and to keep living as we always did is strong, very strong, but now we must be united, even if at a distance, against a common enemy. Infection.
We are neither scientists nor doctors, we are musicians, and during these days we will do what we can to fill your days by sharing with you what happened before this bad news forced us to stop.
But until things change, we invite you, we urge you, and beg you to follow the instructions given by our government and to trust the working experts that day and night are looking for a solution. Our thoughts go to the families of the victims, to all those who fight every day, to heal, to defeat the virus, and to get us back to a normal life."

Måneskin then started their lockdown in Rome, each one on their own. The release of the single *Stato di natura* (*State of Nature*) featuring Francesca Michielin goes almost unnoticed, given the gravity of the situation. And that's a pity because the song is certainly interesting. Francesca raps very relatable things (against catcalling, body-shaming...) and Damiano supports her by talking about toxic masculinity – all under the rock base of the rest of the band. The video, shot in Milan near the vertical forest, looks like an old VHS. At the time, Damiano's relationship with Giorgia Soleri, a fervent feminist, was not known – yet, in the song the private life of Damiano David comes out, he stands out as someone who stops to think and stands for the right causes without ever questioning his identity as a strong person. In December 2020, he will confess to the program *Le Iene* of having said "a few bad things" to a fan that, during a gig, touched Vic's ass. That's an old-fashioned kind of manhood that gets on his nerves. On the other hand, at the Eurovision, Vic said she was lucky to be in a:

"Very good environment, where everyone is really open-minded... if there's someone, like, being rude and stuff they help me and support me, so they don't make me feel like different or..."

"...Wrong," suggests Ethan,

"...So I don't feel like this difference at all – luckily because it should be so for everyone."

We've already met Francesca Michielin several times in this story, as a guest on *X-Factor* and as a host and singer in the Aperol Happy Together event in Venice. She is a friend of Måneskin and she will come back in style, with Fedez, in Sanremo 2021. Yet, this time the band will face her as a rival. Indeed, she has one thing in common with Måneskin: being young and talented, at sixteen she won the fifth edition of *X-*

Factor. She writes her own songs, she was helped in her training by singer-songwriter Elisa and by Fedez, with whom she has been collaborating since 2013. Her song *Amazing* is on the soundtrack of *The Amazing Spiderman 2. Nessun grado di separazione* in 2016 came second at the Sanremo festival, but the winners (the band Stadio) gave up their right to participate in Eurovision, so it was Francesca who went there. Her song was partly translated as *No Degree of Separation*, she ranked sixteenth. After that and during Sanremo 2021, she studied musical composition and in 2022 she participated in the Sanremo Festival as orchestra director for the singer Emma Marrone.

During the lockdown of March and April 2020, from the official Facebook page of Måneskin, they post some backstage clips of the long tour of 2019 to remember the happy days of live shows. Still, in May, a new homemade video came out on the social network: from their four different rooms, Måneskin recorded the cover of *Black Skinhead* by Kanye West feat. Daft Punk. It seems to go back in time to the Måneskin era before *X-Factor,* when the band recorded covers at Vic's. Still, the four of them were happy, technology was finally helping them to keep on working. At that moment, there was nothing else to do, since leaving the house was not allowed. Compared to the old recordings, Måneskin has improved a lot as musicians in those frantic three years.

"I went through two main phases during the lockdown," Damiano said months later to *Billboard:*

"During the first I was really terrified, I used to tell myself: "Oh my God I'm not going out now, I am not doing anything so what do I write?" And I was actually very, very worried and very scared. But then in fact, we all adapted, we started sending each other... guitar riffs, some lyrics... and my brain has blossomed, a completely opposite phase had started. And it was like... in fact, I can't go out, I can't do anything, I'm locked indoors: I have to channel all this energy that I feel into writing, into trying to write new lyrics, into trying to think about new stuff, into trying to change my tone of writing."

"The first obstacle was that we couldn't meet, the four of us together," says Thomas, "but we found our space, each on their own and we were able to influence each other even in a different context." "We found the key," adds Ethan, because in any case:

"It was a difficult moment for everyone, we still had to become aware of the situation we were starting to experience, especially when the lockdown began. So, we also had to think about a new key to approach music, a new approach to writing – by remote."

In May, the first lockdown slowly becomes less strict, then it ended. On May 19, a post appeared on the bands' official Facebook page stating that:

"We are back in the studio, we are finally back together, to rewrite who we are. Our music cannot be made by remote, we need to be together, to look at each other, to confront each other, and to fight even. Today we start to work again on the new album which will be released in 2021.
Beautiful things need time and, above all, we need to be able to bring them in front of you, live.
That's our dimension.

So don't rush, your wait will be much rewarded."

The studio is Ferraguzzo's Il Mulino in the village of Acquapendente. The record is *Teatro d'Ira vol.1*.

Måneskin live through those days by participating in major international events such as the death of George Floyd. On that occasion, the band posts a statement supporting the Black Lives Matter movement on their Facebook page:

"We are living in a critical moment, we all have a duty to act united, for this great cause. Human rights do not depend on any racial or social characteristics. What happened to George Floyd and all the protesters of the #blacklivesmatter cause is irrefutable proof that racism and discrimination against minorities are too entrenched, a scourge in our society. Today it is up to us, no one excluded, to get informed and to fight with all possible means in order to ensure that this abomination won't happen again. So, we ask all of you to take an active part in this cause, by collecting information, by giving and by divulging what is happening (even a small donation can make a difference). We can no longer turn our faces away, saying we are not racist is no longer enough. Ignoring what happens makes you on the oppressor's side. It is up to us to use our privilege to change things, to give a voice to those who are oppressed. We must all unite and fight this battle together for a fairer world."

Immediately under this post there is a picture of Thomas and Damiano kissing, caption goes: *Happy pride*. The four from Monteverde, Rome, have grown – socially-wise.

Summer 2020 in Italy has been an awkward moment of a release of tension after all the madness of spring. We were still wearing masks, but the scorching heat kept the infection curve low. Måneskin recorded their new album, photoshoots were released together with a video in which Damiano cuts his hair. On October 30, the first new single was released, *Vent'anni* (*Twenty years old*). Ethan and Vic had that age, Damiano was twenty-one, Thomas was nineteen. A trailer announced the video, where the four of them, talking in a voice over, reveal their fragile side: Vic's panic attacks, Damiano's fear of being alone, Ethan's fear of not fitting into society, Thomas's introversion. Yet, beyond frailties, there is the desire and the need to make up for the mistakes of those who came first. "Let us love whom we want, let us grow, let us experiment, we want to take the world, we want to change the world, we want to make up for your mistakes, we want to tear down walls," says Damiano. Vic adds: "We want new revolutions, we want colors, we are twenty years old and we will not be silent, and even if you have taught us to hate we will not hate. We are twenty, we are fucking scared – we are twenty and we are afraid of nothing."

Meanwhile, photographer Oliviero Toscani (famous for his Benetton campaigns, among other things) on October 26 takes pictures of Måneskin for the launch of their new single: the band is totally naked. Naked is the soul, naked are the bodies. On Facebook, the caption introducing the picture goes:

"We are ordinary, scared, imperfect human beings.
This is our way to show it, to put our face on it. We stripped completely, we shared our fears, our hopes, our songs.

There are those who will not understand, those who will criticize us, and those who will want to see more deeply. We are twenty years old and this is who we are. Free."

Instagram will immediately censor Vic's naked breasts.

A few days after, *Vent'anni* is performed for the first time by the band in the Colosseum Archaeological Park. It will be used by Sky Sport for an advertisement of Champions League. Vic spoke to *Billboard* about the song:

"In my opinion, it's not easy to speak in such broad terms of a whole generation because it's made of so many different people, that have different personalities, so it is a little difficult to make everyone fit into one opinion. Yet, certainly from many points of view and through many times in any case, in our opinion, today's generation is certainly trying to bring certain matters to light supporting a certain a vision of things... it is trying to aim for better goals, or perhaps to stem all the discrimination that unfortunately exists."

Vent'anni is a poignant and honest ballad about the stage of life through which the four Måneskin members are passing. After the self-affirmation phase, Damiano looks back. He writes a note to himself on the fact that if he makes music and he does it to feel good, not for the money – that is ok, but money is not worth peace of mind which, however, is not there. At twenty years old, the path to peace of mind is made of choices: you can fight or you can run scared, you can blame yourself or others, you can choose to be nice or a bad person. Especially for those who aim "up to the sky," like Måneskin, making the right choices is particularly tough. There is a bit of Italian pop in the chorus of the song, also a bit of old-fashioned rock ballads, especially in Thomas' choices on verse and solo guitar. The song sounds kind of vintage and the video underlines this by alternating a studio part in black and white with a fully colored part that seems to recreate – through cinematography and clothes, like Ethan's flared pink trousers – a certain atmosphere: flower-power, like in the late sixties, early seventies.

Unfortunately, pandemics burst in once again to dampen the band's enthusiasm: in mid-November, Vic and Damiano test covid-positive and are forced to quarantine. Meanwhile, *Billboard Italy* dedicates the November cover to the band, the title is *Rock Education*. In the interview that follows, Damiano states that: "Rock has been the top genre for many years. Its time will surely come again and if we're the first to bring it back, hats off – otherwise we'll be happy anyway." Thomas adds, answering the question: "can rock still conquer the mainstream audience?"

"There is no real recipe to win over the audience, and it's not about playing rock music or not. It is simply all about the fact of being yourself, in a certain sense, and at an artistic level. What we are looking for is to show that here; this world also exists, that is, that of playing analog through musical instruments, that of being a band, that of arousing curiosity; that concerning the desire of a boy of our age, to go to the rehearsal room, buy a guitar and go home with the teacher to study and play. So, we are not trying in a certain sense to conquer that audience, but it's more like: "We are this and we want to show it because it is actually who we are," we are a band and this is our perspective."

"In spite of our genre," says Vic:

> "We live it like this: we try to give our best to create a song that satisfies us and in which we can express ourselves and put what is, in any case, our musical identity. Yet, concerning the genre, the fact that: "rock isn't fashionable anymore," according to us is wrong because... we think it depends on the song, right? I mean, if a song works, if a song is good and people like it, I don't think that people won't listen to it because there is a guitar solo or the sound is rock. Nowadays there's another matter that has to be considered, especially here in Italy, unfortunately, we lost this thing about analog instruments and playing as a band. I mean that, in today's mainstream music there are not many bands. Yet, there's a whole dimension that exists and the fact that it's not promoted does not mean that it cannot work."

During the days of Vic and Damiano's quarantine, *Il ballo della vita* achieves triple platinum. Once the bass and voice get better, the band shoots a vlog in which Thomas asks Alexa to: "Say hello to the Måneskin." "Hey!" Replies the lamp, "it's Måneskin, yeah!" About the new single, the lamp comments: "You are finally back. My circuits have already learned it by heart." When Damiano asks who the biggest fan of Måneskin is, the lamp proudly states: "Modestly, I know all your songs."

Vent'anni turns gold just before Christmas. At the end of November, the band plays the song at X-Factor Italy. Around Christmas, Måneskin announce that they will take part in the Sanremo Festival. Then, on December 25, Damiano's butt, with the "Kiss this" tattoo on his left cheek, acts as a

Christmas tree in the greeting card on the band's social media.

Part 5.

Sanremo 2021

W hat is the Sanremo Festival? Tough question! Well... it's a festival, the most important Italian festival concerning mainstream music. It started after the war to relaunch tourism – and the Casino – in the town of Sanremo, near the border with France. The Sanremo Festival has penetrated so deeply into Italian culture that it is not just a singing competition, but a kind of barometer to the pulse of what is happening in the nation at a political, economic, social and cultural level. Anyone who goes to the Sanremo Festival is known by everyone for about a week. They become famous – or they already are.

Domenico Modugno, that of *Volare* (the real title of the song is *Nel blu dipinto di blu*) started from Sanremo in 1958. Nine years later the singer-songwriter Luigi Tenco died mysteriously after the first evening of the Festival – a weird, unlikely, and never thoroughly investigated suicide that didn't succeed in stopping the 1967 edition of the Festival. Yet, it deeply shocked public opinion. So much so that the generation of songwriters and rockers (mainly prog rock) of the seventies, avoided Sanremo; sometimes putting on counter-festivals to protest against the commercial exploitation of music without caring much about the quality of the songs, against briberies, bets, and corruption, and against a certain moralistic and political censorship.

Within the decade, 1973-1978 was in absolute decadence for the Festival, from 1975 television only broadcasted the final evening. During the eighties, however, the competition flourished again, so much so that they could afford international guests: the likes of Peter Gabriel (who thumped his back against the stage in a reckless performance of *Shock the monkey*), Queen; who, angry at the imposed playback, performed *Radio GaGa* unveiling the trick during the 1984 edition, or the long-awaited Duran Duran in 1985 which caused scenes of mass hysteria that, in Italy, we haven't seen since the Beatles.

The Festival used to take place at the Casino, now the location is the Ariston Theatre.

Sanremo is notorious for having a conservative audience devoted to the Italian melodic song style, a limit that the last two artistic directions (one of the singer Claudio Baglioni the other of the host and former DJ Amadeus) have attempted to force. Baglioni opened up to rap, Amadeus balanced old melodic singers, rappers, indie pop, and finally rock, which maybe is the more absent genre in the whole history of the Festival. In the seventies, rockers wanted to keep a distance, mainly for political reasons, after the seventies rock was considered 'not suitable' for Sanremo anyway. If we think about the words: 'rock' and 'Sanremo' put together, we can't help thinking about Placebo, who participated as special guests in 2001: they performed *Special K*, Brian Molko then smashed an amplifier with his guitar, the audience booed them. In many ways, Sanremo seems the antithesis of rock.

Yet, some rock musicians have been there. Some PFM members took part in the 1988 edition with a crazy side-project (in fact, it even included three comedians) called *I figli di Bubba* (*Sons of Bubba*). Then – not joking this time – Afterhours took part in the 2009 edition, with a song that called for political action in the stagnant cultural atmosphere of Italy at the end of the 2000s. Manuel Agnelli, we know him by now, didn't care about the competition: instead, he just wanted to launch a compilation album with the same title as the Afterhours Sanremo song: *Il paese è reale* (*The nation is real*), that included nineteen interesting underground artists.

Many controversies preceded the 2021 edition of Sanremo: on one side there were those who believed that the Festival should be stopped due to the gravity of the pandemic situation, on the other there were those who pointed out that the Italian music industry is already in crisis and, given that it is mainly based on Sanremo, the show had to go on – safely. Those controversies move the festival by about a month, pushing it to March. Finally, a compromise was reached: the Festival took place without an audience. The orchestra was set up in such a way that it also served as the audience. Amadeus, the host but also the artistic director, seemed comfortable with the idea, that on the other hand bothered his friend and co-host Fiorello (in whose radio show Måneskin have already been guests twice), who is used to having feedback from the room all the time.

No audience and curfew: if they are not at work, singers must return to their hotel by ten. Orietta Berti, the melodic singer who looks like a sweet granny, whom we met in Zurich with Måneskin, is chased by the police because she had gone to pick up her clothes for the stage just after ten in the evening! In the same edition, she will flood her hotel room and will declare wanting to collaborate with "the Naziskins," blatantly mistaking the name of Måneskin, and winning the award for most transgressive singer off-stage.

In addition to Orietta, among the participants there are: Ghemon, the author of *Un temporale* the song that made it hard for Damiano at *X Factor*, Colapesce and Di Martino with their incredibly catchy song *Musica leggerissima* (*Super-light music*), the glam performer Achille Lauro and above all there is Fedez, who turns from judge to direct rival for Måneskin. He sings *Chiamami per nome* (*Call me by name*) paired with his longtime friend Francesca Michielin and, with that brilliant way of managing social media, his partner Chiara Ferragni certainly helps in influencing the audience's vote. Fedez and Michielin are certainly the most formidable opponents of Måneskin this time. But besides, being opponents, they are also friends. Victoria says on Instagram that, if they don't win, she'd like "Franci, our *friendie*" to win.

Måneskin are there because Amadeus, as artistic director of the Festival, chose them. Since the singer Diodato won the festival the previous year with *Fai rumore* (*You're my sound in the background*), a poignant melodic ballad about a love that ends (probably dedicated to his former companion, Levante), the presence of Måneskin at the Festival confuses their fan base a little. Most of them expected something like *Torna a casa* from them. In hindsight, knowing that *Teatro d'Ira* was ready, one would think that they could have presented a ballad – like *Vent'anni* – releasing *Zitti e buoni* later. That would have been acting in accordance with the Festival's taste. But this is Måneskin, shocking and teasing is in their DNA – so much so that, before getting into the contest, they left their *Twitter* page in the hands of the satirical account @Dio. They would have disappointed their public, then, if they had sung some ballad or anything that could be defined as 'suitable for Sanremo.' Their fan base began to understand that the song, of which only the title was known (the Sanremo songs must be unreleased), was not a ballad when the band described it to *RaiPlay* as follows:

"The song we'll perform is called *Zitti e buoni*, and it is mainly about redemption and the desire to break the world with music. (...) The sound of the song is currently a mystery, but we can say that it is perfectly in Måneskin's style."

During the first live Instagram feed, Damiano said: "The song was so wrong that we said 'Cool! Let's do Sanremo!'" In fact, on the first evening, the jury composed of a sample of the population (called *giuria demoscopica*), taken by surprise, rewards the singer-songwriter Annalisa Scarrone. Måneskin classify seventh, Fedez and Michielin fourth. The music critic Ernesto Assante, however, in the newspaper *La Repubblica* gives the band a vote of 9/10, arguing that: "Electricity and conscience, power and control. In a word: rock. How it was, how it is, how it will be."

Sanremo has changed the procedure of voting many times. On the last three editions, juries were made of three types: one of professionals, one *demoscopic* and the last one composed of people at home, televoting.

"We tried to enjoy our performance," Vic told *Cosmopolitan:* "Actually, before getting on stage we told ourselves: 'it's like being in the rehearsal room,' let's go there and let's enjoy it." If, on the other hand, during the first performance, Damiano often looks down and does not seem to calculate the orchestra – that is the audience – that's because during rehearsals there was a camera on the floor. Yet, that evening, the director decided to keep it off. "I thought I was super intense, but instead I was watching the floor," comments the front-man. As for the other artists competing, during the interview with *Cosmo*, Måneskin send hearts to Orietta Berti. Damiano then said to the magazine *Amica* that Orietta had personally apologized to the band for calling them Naziskin but that they, who have taken it laughing, love her even more after that. In their personal preferences there is the singer-songwriter Max Gazzè from Rome, the rapper-songwriter Madame and the singer Gaia (of whom Damiano says, "We had the same dress, I was in black she was in white").

Actually, Amadeus was co-hosting and Fiorello had the comic relief role. Five 'alpha women' (as *Cosmo* defined them) – the actress Matilda De Angelis (no relation to Vic), the singer Elodie, the conductor Beatrice Venezi, the journalist Barbara Palombelli and the model Vittoria Ceretti – joined them onstage, co-hosting in turns, from evening to evening. "We have many talented professionals," comments Damiano on that, "and it is right that we begin to recognize them and we must not always have men in places of power and in places of relevance because it is rather ridiculous, in our opinion."

Although not too gifted from a technical point of view ("we are huge boomers," says Damiano), Måneskin do some live feeds on Instagram like they used to at *X-Factor*, before going onstage, to keep the fan base warm. Ethan confesses he is excited – but obviously, it doesn't show – about the band's debut at the Ariston Theatre. According to others, his style has somehow turned into a more 'metal' way of playing, louder than usual – especially when it comes to cymbals. "He plays the drums very loud," says Vic, "all sweaty, with the faces he makes." In a second live feed on Instagram (where there's also Vic's dog, Chili), Damiano defines the town of Sanremo as "*bella fracica*" (which is roman dialect for "rottenly beautiful," as in drenched in beauty), while Vic admits she is the most anxious of the band and answers the question: "Will you win Sanremo?" "No, we will come seconds again." Instead, Thomas admits that, in an interview, he gave an old-school rocker answer. The question was: "What will you do tomorrow?" The answer (as if Thomas had grown with the old generations of amplifiers) was: "We'll turn on the tubes!" Some annoying fan asks if Marlena has finally come back home.

The second evening was dedicated to the artists who hadn't performed on the first day – the singer-songwriter and rapper Irama, who's in quarantine, is replaced by the video of his audition that he did months before, because it is now clear that he will not be able to leave the hotel.
For some years now, during the Festival, one night is devoted to covers: the competing artists have to perform existing songs of their choice, often (but not always) in a duet with others, and by 'others' I mean other singers, other actors, other show professionals not involved in the competition. That of the covers is a separate competition that has nothing to do with the main one.
It was the third evening and Måneskin show up with another song not really suitable for Sanremo, the cover of *Amandoti* (*Loving you*) – a ballad-tango – originally written by a band called CCCP, punk/post-rock and absolutely underground. "It took a long time to choose a song that could represent us

and that could be rearranged to our mood, respecting the core of it," explains Damiano to *Cosmopolitan:*

> "So, when this song came to mind, we realized – I really think from the first rehearsal – that it was the one, because it actually sounded right to us, we played it very well, melodically for me it was very nice to sing, I enjoy it, I like it, I also like how we play it hence bit by bit the choice became obvious."

There is only one person who can go back to the Sanremo stage and sing *Amandoti* with Damiano for the occasion: Manuel Agnelli, the old mentor. For Damiano, once they chose the song, choosing the guest was 'straightforward.' Manuel for Damiano: "is perfect, as we wanted to respect the importance of the song: that it's the history of rock and we needed... a rock historian. Then the fact that we are friends also counts." Manuel Agnelli had already expressed himself on *Zitti e buoni*, complaining to the newspaper *La Stampa* that there were many interesting artists at the Festival who dared little and conformed to Sanremo standards for fear of losing visibility. "In my opinion, it's just the other way round," he said: "if you bring something that does not conform to the Sanremo Festival's usual standards, it can make a lot more sense and maybe you can gain even more visibility – that's what I hope for Måneskin."

On the night of the covers, under the direction of Maestro Enrico Melozzi, the four Måneskin members, wearing *new romantic* shirts and corsets, faced a bare-chested Manuel Agnelli, vaguely dressed like a samurai. The tango-punk duet that followed, eye to eye with Damiano, was incredibly intense and supported by Thomas's solo, by the interlocking between Agnelli's rhythmic guitar, Vic's bass and by Ethan's drum hits. Songwriter Ermal Meta won the night of the covers, but Måneskin impressed the audience. In the week of Sanremo, the *Amandoti* video was the most clicked on the Rai platform. Ernesto Assante got excited and gave them a nice 9/10 again.

"We understood that something was in the air," Damiano told the newspaper *Il Fatto Quotidiano*, "on the night of the covers – there was such an enthusiastic response from the audience that... anyway we knew we made it a step further."

During the fifth evening, Amadeus scrolls the provisional results. Måneskin are initially in fifth place: first is Ermal Meta, given as the favorite. During the grand finale, Måneskin perform wearing the nude suit signed Etro. They voted once to decide the podium, mixing the result to those of the previous evenings. The vote ended up like this: Ermal Meta in the third position, Fedez and Michielin came first, then we have Måneskin coming in second. If the Festival had stopped there, the rapper and the songwriter would have certainly won. However, there is a second round of votes. Televoting turns crucial for Måneskin and, given the 10% gap that separated them from Fedez and Michielin, they won. Since Fedez's wife is the queen of influencers, winning was not easy. It is the evening of March 6, 2021.

When Amadeus breaks the news, the four Måneskin members, Fedez and Michielin are all hugging together. Damiano starts to cry and hugs Ethan. Vic lets herself go, swearing. When they ask them to play the song once again, according to regulations, she exclaims "Oh shit!" The newspapers incorrectly report it as: "No shit!" – but the effect is funny.

In a live Instagram feed a few hours later, the band keeps repeating: "How the fuck did this happen?" While Damiano is looping: "I have no words, I have no words, thank you." Thomas does not rationalize it: "It is something that is not making sense." None of them, of course, expected it; neither does the whole of Italy. And who knows if Fedez, while clapping his hands, thought about that evening during the audition on September 21, 2017, when he said yes, that he was opening the path for a band that was now blowing him away to take first prize in Sanremo.

The press conference, which usually takes place late at night, is postponed until the next day, with the artists on videoconference and the journalists keeping social distances. Some of them, like *the Newsic* correspondent, complained that the sound was awful.

Damiano warmly declares, regarding his tears: "Some think that we are machines and that we just play and we don't have feelings, but we are human beings and we have feelings and with this victory, we realized that we have done something important." On Chiara Ferragni's support for Fedez, he says: "They have a child together, it is obvious that Fedez and Chiara Ferragni support each other, it is the same thing that all families do. All this complaining is pointless." Concerning the album yet to be released, Vic and Thomas tell the press that they were mainly influenced by the London rock scene. On playing with the orchestra, Vic says:

"Maestro Enrico Melozzi was excellent, it was incredible, being able to play with sixty elements. He had the idea of the standing orchestra, some of them said they enjoyed playing our song. We are musicians, we do not feel like giving advice to anyone but this working sector, that is vital, it's suffered a lot in this period. We hope this message can be a sign of recovery."

The bassist alludes to the covid situation that has penalized many sectors, such as the musical one, that already had many issues to overcome before the pandemics. Damiano also thanks the conductor of the orchestra, maestro Enrico Melozzi.

"We brought this song because it is the perfect representation of who we are now, of our current sound," the singer adds, "we brought our identity, it's also an unconventional piece. We did not expect such a fast reception from the public. We brought something different. The victory made us understand that the general response was very positive." "I'm happy and dazed," adds Fedez, "it was a wonderful experience. Backstage, it was great to be together with Måneskin."

Meanwhile, Manuel Agnelli takes it as a personal victory. The day after the sixth and final night, he declared to *Rockol*: "My adrenaline is still running, I was up all night." He calls the televoting gap that made Måneskin win: "the real victory" and admits he is surprised:

> "I expected them to have good results, you could see that they had a certain amount of energy and freshness that the others didn't have. But could Måneskin win...? I didn't dare believe it. Yet, after the cover we did together, I realized how much attention there was around these guys."

On how he found the band, he says:

"I found them grown up and aware that they are passing through a crucial moment in their career. They are focused, busy, they work a lot, even in the rehearsal room: there they don't need any advice. Instead, I advised them not to take their talent for granted: the risk is to stop and settle. They are in their twenties now; they have to grow up and they don't have to settle. They don't have to work on details so much, but on content, they have to become more and more interesting."

In addition to Manuel, whom is personally involved in the success of the band, there is Vasco Rossi, a rocker and songwriter who, on the Sanremo stage in 1983, presented his most iconic song entitled *Vita spericolata* (*Reckless life* – in the song he yells that he wants "a life like Steve McQueen's, a life full of troubles") obviously positioning second last. Those were the days when rock and Sanremo didn't get along. Vasco, who is super-famous now; his gigs need the space of a stadium, doesn't hide his support for Måneskin from his social networks. After the final night of Sanremo, he sends his compliments to the band. In October, he will say: "I like them very much. It's like watching myself again when I started: same energy." After the Eurovision, he compared *Zitti e buoni* to his generational anthem *Siamo solo noi* (*It's just us*):

"The song was great – the opening riff is phenomenal. In my opinion, it's a riff that suits a great rock song. When I heard the lyrics that say: "We are out of our minds, but different from them," it's seemed to me like that is their *Siamo solo noi*. I felt that sense of rebellion, they have the same desire to go against the conformism of society that I felt. Today there's another kind of conformism – perhaps it's worse – through the various social networks where the craziest things often triumph, from the Flat Earth Society to those who wrote to me saying that I invited everyone to put on masks because I was afraid of the virus."

A few days later in a relaxed interview with Stefano Fisico – the same one in which Vic laughs herself to tears for having granted the wish of his uncle Andrea, who wished to be mentioned for people who didn't believe that Vic was his niece – Damiano speaks up and gives the actual answer to the question: "How do you feel about winning the Sanremo festival?"

"How the fuck do I have to feel? I am twenty-two; this one is twenty, we won Sanremo Festival, with all due respect; how do I have to feel? [ironically/sarcastically] I feel shit! I'm terribly sick, I haven't slept in a week since it happened, because I didn't like it."

But 2021 doesn't end here for Måneskin. This was only the beginning.

Part 6.

From Rotterdam to the world

I just want to say to Måneskin:
go to Rotterdam, break their asses
and bring the award to Italy.
[Ermal Meta,
press conference
after Sanremo]

D uring the last press conference, Måneskin confirm that they will represent Italy at the Eurovision Song Contest, a privilege of those who win the Festival. Francesca Michielin, who had already been to the ESC, will declare at the press conference: "Pieces of Advice to Måneskin for the ESC? They don't need this. Being part of the ESC is beautiful, it is a moment of pure madness."
Usually, the long Sunday show on Rai1, *Domenica In*, the day after Sanremo does a live special, not from TV studios but from the Ariston theater itself. On March 7, 2021, one of the historical hosts of *Domenica In*, Mara Venier (dubbed "aunt Mara"), is the first to have the band as guests on the show. She herself agrees that the victory was unexpected. The four Måneskin members in this interview are funny: they all stand close together on one side of the stage, as if Venier – who represents the top of the Italian mainstream media – embarrasses them a little. "It's the first time," says Damiano,

"we're not used to it." *Domenica in* is not like *Che tempo che fa*: Fabio Fazio's TV program has a certain intellectual open-minded target, *Domenica in* is for everybody. Actor and singer Claudio Santamaria, present in the studio, defines them as: "The right epilogue of a revolution that began in 2009 with Afterhours, with Manuel Agnelli who is their 'spiritual father'... then the Zen Circus came, together with Motta..." (Other names of the Italian underground that went to Sanremo) Speaking of Manuel, live on air, Mara sends the reply of *Amandoti* that moved her particularly. The journalist Giovanna Botteri, who in 2020 closely followed the start of the covid nightmare, is also a guest on the show and she says (perhaps centering the reasons of the unexpected fortune of *Zitti e buoni*): "We're out of our minds, we're all out of our minds! After a year we all feel rock, we are all pissed off, we are all full of energy: this is this year's song." "For me, they are... The Rolling Stones," concludes Mara Venier, "but there is a woman!"

That same evening, Måneskin are Fabio Fazio's guests at *Che tempo che fa?* There to once again play *Zitti e buoni*, all dressed in white. The resident comedian of the show, Luciana Littizzetto, speaks for everyone when she notices the energy of the band despite a week in Sanremo. "You don't wanna do this song first on gigs; otherwise, you'll collapse!" She says, to which Damiano replies: "Soon the record will come out, and the other songs are even worse." Vic confesses that she slept; "About ten minutes," Damiano explains that interviews lasted until half-past four in the morning. Littizzetto also notes that finally Thomas Raggi, who doesn't smile much, smiled too. Fabio Fazio, in videoconference due to covid, confirms his support for the band and claims that he had recognized years earlier how much the band was an absolute novelty in the Italian scene. Speaking of Vic's "oh shit!" at the awards ceremony, Luciana Littizzetto (often accused of putting too many bad words in her monologues) declares: "in fact, I am totally at ease with them, indeed if you need some advice, some cards, some new bad words, you know that I am really very talented at this."

Soon after Sanremo the new tour dates come out: Måneskin now play in arenas and sports halls, the maximum they can get in terms of the amplitude of venues. Rome's gig needs another date and Milan is sold out in less than six hours – eleven days after the festival it will be necessary to triple it. *Zitti e buoni* already had 1,300,000 Spotify streams in one day. "We can't wait to be back on stage," Damiano declares to *Il Fatto Quotidiano*:

> "Furthermore, we are looking forward to meeting up with our entire team of technicians, engineers, etc. again because, in any case, as people who work behind the scenes; clearly they don't have the same exposure as us, but if we can do what we can do – tours, concerts – It's mainly thanks to them and I don't think we would be able to put up a stage."

Now that the band is popular on national territory – *really* popular – futile quarrels concerning rock identity start: are Måneskin a rock band? Aren't they? If not, what's their genre? Etc... Meanwhile, the video of *Zitti e buoni*, with that slight nineties patina that makes it look like a sort of "austerity-version" of the *Adore* video by the Smashing Pumpkins (who, by the way, had a woman playing bass until 2010), is released.

In the nineties and early aughts, the leading Italian rock bands were Afterhours and Marlene Kuntz. Marlene Kuntz's singer, Cristiano Godano, speaks his mind on Måneskin from the pages of *Rolling Stone Italy*. The article he wrote is about Måneskin, but begins as a lucid analysis of the generational gap. Godano writes about his son Enrico, who is also a musician:

> "What amazed me and never ceases to amaze me is this incredible attraction to the matter of competition. To the concept of competing. It is an ingredient that, among many, clearly shows the generational gap between two ideas of music: mine, linked to a pure artistic ideal that knows how to do without – with brazen awareness – muscular performance aimed at the inclusive success of the implication of wealth; and his, completely connected to what these competitions – at least in appearance – promise, that is an immediate stellar success made of sudden universal recognition and a profusion of euros, without the purgatorial scourge of the so-called apprenticeship and the long and slow path made of bone-breaking concerts in small, dirty and disorganized clubs."

The new generations are more pragmatic, they are not ashamed of using the means of capitalism (competition, mainstream language) because they perceive that, in addition to living with music today, they need to think about making a living from it tomorrow.

The front-man of Marlene Kuntz however, at a certain point turns towards the famous controversy about rock, called into question on Instagram by a fan, of which he: "perceived clearly that she was one of those who do not praise them, and gave reasons... such as: 'the front-man shows off so much, as if he were the reincarnation of Cobain,' bringing humility as a value into this." Less visceral than Manuel Agnelli, but coming from the same generation and with the same competence in the matter, Godano intelligently replies:

"Måneskin are a rock band, are they not? And what would you like them to do, if they are not a rock band for you? Of course, they are a rock band. It's pop-rock, though. All their language is pop. The way they communicate is grafted onto the language of television, on which they depend and which they know how to exploit to a great extent... They do rock and they do it well, I mean they play it well, they have their unmistakable sound, they are badass on stage, they have style, and that's no small thing. They tend towards a glam attitude; they are light years away from the nerds of indie rock... and their aptitude is a bit of a crossover, but with a Led Zeppelin aftertaste via Greta Van Fleet in the background.... They are a product of a commercial nature, they achieve success after success, they wink at the mainstream, they seek it, they find it, and this is probably their most serious "fault," which causes widespread gnawing.

Many Italian musicians have expressed themselves in favor of them after the Sanremo performance, because as musicians, they feel as I feel, that these guys rock. It is not for everyone to go to the Ariston stage and do the right thing: they did it. Their expressed anger was credible (but functional to success, mind you, therefore credible in its unavoidable artifice), they rendered it with an adequate aesthetic, each of them is a character in itself (I love the guitarist: isn't he a crazy fellow?). The timbre of their instruments is rock, their sound is set on a bass-guitar-drums line-up, their grand riffs belong to the rock of all time, their rhythms as well.

All these are rock ingredients. And among the rock ingredients, I don't understand why for many there must be humility. I don't want our fan to resent me, yet she expressed her concept of rock relying on very specific values (which I know well, they belong to me in a consubstantial way), including a non-excessive attitude and a preponderant poetic-intellectual component (what did I let you guess about Måneskin above? No difficult or depressing concepts, just youth and coolness). But, and this is the first band that comes to me at random, could one ever have expected humility from Oasis? Humility and Oasis: don't you think these are two terms in strong contradiction? Or from the Stones when they were young? ... (please, do not get annoyed dear fan: after all, you have no idea how many: "Godano shows off so much," I got in life and here on the net, directly and indirectly, yet I don't show off, and you know it, and our fans know it) But going on stage and "acting cool" is the quintessence of rock: even getting on stage with that fake carelessness of a nerdy attitude is a way to "look cool" on stage."

And more:

"Then I am asked to speak my mind on rock music coming back to win. Hmm. I'll say it again, I don't like that kind of rock very much, but the song is not bad at all... If it helped make people want rock and guitars back, I could only be very happy about it. Will it happen? Won't happen? I have no idea. But I sure hope it will. Because hoping is worth it, like having faith."

Meanwhile on Facebook, Drusilla Foer – a cultivated and elegant female character and alter ego of the actor Gianluca Gori (in 2022 she will be chosen as the third fluid female presence of the Festival), comments below a video of the recordings of the vocal parts of *Zitti e buoni:* "How beautiful. Aunt Dru."

On March 15, nine days before the end of Sanremo, *Zitti e buoni* turns gold. *Teatro d'ira* is expected on March 19. The title of the album comes from: "the passion, anger, and determination that we carry in every note of our songs." They don't repress anger, they transferred it into their music. On Facebook, they briefly describe the new songs. Besides *Vent'anni*, *Zitti e buoni* and *Coraline*, of which we will talk about later, there is *Graffi sui gomiti* (*Bruises on the elbows*), a classic rock song with a wide guitar riff, described as: "a story of revenge, a slap in the face to whoever has doubted us and our abilities, a hymn of revenge."

As we understand by now, Måneskin are not just four rock stars seeking glory but four human beings with their frailties that are, at times, paralyzing – Vic's panic attacks, Ethan's difficulties in integrating, Thomas's introversion, Damiano's fears. Their generation is that of precocious bullies, but also that of inclusion: it's acceptable not to conform to the cultural standard. As for Damiano, one can redeem oneself by refusing to follow the traditional middle-class attitude based on contempt: "of those who have less than you, as those who are above, praise them / honor your mother and father but spit on them behind their back / but I still have my way, the glancing, three friends who are not cowards." Then, there is *I Wanna Be Your Slave*, Damiano's favorite song of the album, where Thomas and Vic dub the voice winking at eighties dance music and good old glam rock – the hint is enough to gain the attention of one of the protagonists and survivors of that era, Iggy Pop. They describe the piece as: "Sex, in all its forms and from every angle, the antinomy that lives in all of us and makes us human, imperfect, sinful and in need of redemption."

Nel nome del padre (*In the name of the Father*) follows on the track list. It is about the 'sacred' importance of music. Damiano exposes his fears – the fear of feeling perpetually unsatisfied in the first place, given the overwhelming pressure of the life he leads. Being famous is not only about money, it is something you have to maintain through hard work and sacrifices (first, you have to give up a part of your private life). Being famous exposes you in such ways that any of those gossiping, envying and hating, would probably never accept. "Success is not a costly necklace or a wristwatch to show off and prove that you have made it," writes Mattia Marzi on *Rockol*, "But an amulet to chase away certain ghosts of the past." The band no longer needs Marlena to talk about this. "If the old album is more metaphorical," Vic said to *Il Fatto Quotidiano*, "Here we are just brutally honest." Damiano is so angry that he almost raps ("You stay an inch from my ass, you dickhead!"), Vic supports him with a melodic bass line – she likes what in Italy is called 'basso cantante,' 'singing bass' like the instrument is whistling a melody.

Then there is *For your love*, which has the same title of a well-known piece by the Yardbirds. Thomas starts with a guitar riff; the interlocking sounds are remarkably interesting – bass and guitar keep "singing" melodies during the verse. Maybe that's the song where Thomas and Vic stand out the most, it's probably here where the echoes of a certain experience, that refers to the London underground scene, are best recognizable. From Facebook, the band describes this song as: "An alcoholic evening, love at first sight, possession, and obsession. A toxic relationship between the protagonist and his muse. For your love, I will do whatever you want."

At the end of the track list, there is *La paura del buio* (*Fear of the dark*), which almost takes up the title of the iconic Afterhours album *Hai paura del buio?* On Facebook, it's described as follows: "It is the story of the conflictual relationship between the artist and music, which is a disease and the cure. An imposing presence that, at times, takes your breath away and at others, allows you to breathe."

Teatro d'ira is definitely a rockier album than *Il ballo della vita*. No concessions here to trap or reggaeton. The band sought after a certain vintage sound, recorded live at the Il Mulino studio, utilizing the tube amps that Thomas likes so much, plus the analog banks. Måneskin thus demonstrates that they have internalized the post-modern lesson: making old clothes new, without seeking a supposed total originality that is perhaps an illusion. Even the cover photo of the album is reminiscent of the classics of rock, such as *Who's next* from the Who.

Some questionable reviews come out, like that of Claudio Todesco in *Rolling Stone Italy*. It seems that he is missing the fact that Måneskin are rock, but they are also mainstream. Todesco dislikes the 'staged anger' of the record – yet, staging emotions was in the stylistic code of rockstars such as David Bowie, and that the anger is 'theatrical' is also stated in the title of the album. Todesco also does not like it when Damiano David's vocals are over the top: he compares him to the melodic lack of sophistication of singer Emma Marrone – yet Steve Tyler sang like this, Axl Rose as well, let's talk about that... In conclusion, with a little touch of inferiority complex, congenital to the Italian rock critic, the journalist writes that when Damiano sings in English, Måneskin turns into a second-rate band – this was obviously before the international success and the intercession of Iggy Pop and Mick Jagger.

On *Rock Shock* Michele Larotonda's review is better. However, he feels the need to put the disclaimer on his words of appreciation:

> "I may not be very popular, but these days when we just hear rap, trap, autotune, and stuff like that, the new Måneskin album – *Teatro d'ira Volume 1* - it's a healthy breath of fresh air, of honest and healthy rock, made with real instruments."

Antonio Silvestri's on *Onda rock,* goes further:

> "If we want to analyze it as an ordinary album, then, *Teatro d'ira – vol. 1* was released by a quartet of very young people in love with the rock of twenty or thirty years ago; Damiano David's voice stands out, he is the band's restless and talented front-man. They are capable of shaking with some thunderous, though still very formulaic, guitar *riffs*. They can move, although still with painful pathetic overtones, in the most intimate moments. They are ambitious, and perhaps the *Teatro d'ira* project will give us something more solid to imagine their future."

On March 26, *Teatro d'ira* is at the top of the charts. *Zitti e buoni* will have gone platinum five times – just the very catchy *Musica leggerissima* of Colapesce and Di Martino, among the songs of Sanremo, will do the same on the Italian market. Vic gets photographed unfiltered for the cover of *Elle*, to promote beauty without the need for apps or app filters – a need that is a symptom of insecurity, Vic herself has struggled a lot with it. Orietta Berti, meanwhile, on a TV show entitled *Name that tune,* accepts the challenge of mimicking Damiano's moves in the *Zitti e buoni* video and of performing the song in lip-sync with the original tune. When the newspaper *Il Fatto Quotidiano* asks Måneskin who they would have liked to win Sanremo if they hadn't, the band replies almost in sync 'Orietta Berti,' who in turn, declares that Ethan is her favorite of the band.

When Damiano is asked if it's true that Italy is not a country for young people, he replies: "The future is always in the hands of young people, so it becomes for young people when young people decide to take it."

The Eurovision Song Contest takes place between May 18-22, in Rotterdam, as Dutch singer Duncan Lawrence won the 2019 edition. In 2020, due to covid, ESC was canceled, preventing Diodato – winner of Sanremo 2020 – from participating. In 2021, Australia and Israel were also competing. As explained by Eugenio Ceriello of *Radio Stonata* in an extremely useful tutorial, there are thirty-nine competing countries and everyone sings on pre-recorded background music. Six countries have the right to enter the contest directly at the final. They are: the host country and the so-called Big Five (Germany, France, Spain, United Kingdom, and Italy), which are the five countries that contribute most to the EBU (The European Broadcasting Union), a company which gathers together all the public TV channels of Europe that organize the competition. As for the other thirty-three countries, they have to compete in two semifinals, ten of them will pass the round. At the final stage, there are twenty-six countries left. Each of them has two juries: one is at home televoting, and the other is composed by professionals. From home, one can vote for anyone except one's own country (country code of telephone numbers shall prevail). The sum of the votes from both juries determines the winner.

Among the other participants, the Belgian Hooverphonic have been known for the hit *Mad about you*, released the year Ethan and Vic were born. Twenty years later, singer Geike Arnaert looks stunningly like Cate Blanchett. The French contestant, on the other hand, is Barbara Pravi, who participates with an old-style *chanson*, *Voilà*. Pre-ESC preparations begin at the end of April: the Spain pre-party is the first event at which Måneskin take part, live from home. On May 11, on the band's Facebook page, it's reported that the four have "Landed in Rotterdam." Unfortunately, due to the covid restrictions, Damiano, Vic, Thomas, and Ethan cannot visit the city or leave their hotel. The Arena, however, is beautiful. The front-man and the guitar player describe it as a space shuttle, like the Enterprise. The first run-through, amidst the fireworks of the scenography, is on May 13. The second rehearsal is on May 15. A YouTube user writes: "if Måneskin win, it would be a legendary Eurovision moment." On May 18, – the day when Franco Battiato, a particularly important songwriter, died – the competition begins. Måneskin, by regulation, enter at the final stage of it.

During the second Big Five press conference, presented by Samya Hafsaoui, a Danish journalist focuses on the band's sophisticated look, then asks: "If you win, can we claim a quote about that, Victoria?" "Of course," she replies. Denmark did not qualify that year. "I am also very proud to represent Denmark in this competition as well," the bassist told *Good Evening Europe*, Denmark's biggest ESC news site. Back to the press conference, a Polish journalist says that he received more questions from home for Måneskin than the other competitors. According to a British journalist, they are the second favorites to win. Despite this, Vic wants to clarify that what the band wants is not so much to win, but to: 'share our music.' Like journalist Giovanna Botteri said, his British colleague agrees that *Zitti e buoni* was successful because: "during the pandemic we needed all this energy." It is at this press conference that the band is selected to play during the second half of the program.

In an informal interview, from *wiwibloggs*, the reporter tells Damiano: "I didn't recognize you because you're wearing clothes." The joke then turns into a question on gender rules: "oftentimes in movies and TV shows, it's sort of the women who are said... they're told 'please take your clothes off' but here it's reversed." "The way that we dress is very against, like, maybe, gender norms about how you should wear and how you should dress... Boys shouldn't wear makeup and stuff... So we do it also to give a message of freedom," Vic promptly replies. They are then asked if in the Italian industry they felt like outsiders, the answer is definitely yes, from the beginning to Sanremo, "but we don't mind it a lot," says Damiano. "I was ready to rip my t-shirt off," the British interviewer from *Eurovoxx* then tells them, to show how much they "rocked the Arena" during rehearsals. In the same interview, it turns out that off stage "Thomas is the wildest one," Er Cobbra confesses that once he drove on the shore of Lake Martignano at four in the morning with his car.

Meanwhile, one of the vocalists of the Serbian girl band Hurricane, Sanja, admits in a press conference that she has a crush on Damiano – Hurricane even sing the refrain of *Zitti e buoni a cappella* in harmony. "He is a beautiful man. It's platonic... I mean, I am single... I know basically, I would like to marry him" says the brunette of the trio, six years older than the front-man.

Before the final night of ESC, Måneskin do not lose their good habits: they go live on Instagram for their followers. Only this time, it's their first in English. The band films the backstage of the Eurovision: the hairdressers, the delegations, but above all the ping pong table where Damiano, who still is a sporty guy, has beaten many.

During the final night, many countries have pop-dance vocalists singing in English to represent them – Elena Tsagrinou (Cyprus), Eden Alene (Israel) Destiny (Malta), Stefania (Greece), Natalia Gordienko (Moldova), Efendi (Azerbaijan), Tusse (Sweden), Senhit (San Marino). A few pop-dance vocalists sing in their own language – Anxela Peristeri (Albania), Hurricane (Serbia). Then there are male vocalists: The Black Mamba (Portugal), James Newman for the United Kingdom (who will score zero points total), Blas Cantò for Spain, The Roop for Lithuania, TIX for Norway, Jeangu Macrooy for Holland and Gjon's Tears for Switzerland (French-speaking side). Then there are the funny performances – Manizha, dressed as a Russian doll, and Jendrik with his ukulele from Germany – as well as the original performances of the intimistic Victoria, a kind of Francesca Michielin from Bulgaria, and Barbara Pravi's *chanson* for France. Ukraine's band stands out: it's called Go_a and is a folktronica group, therefore very influenced by traditional music in terms of voice, rhythm, and electronic versions of traditional instruments such as flutes. In addition to the already mentioned Hooverphonic, the other bands are the electro-dance group Daði og Gagnamagnið from Iceland (who had some covid problems) and the Blind Channel from Finland, the only other rock band, metal actually. After all, the last rock group to win Eurovision was a Suomi formation, it was in 2006 and the band was Lordi. In the second press conference, Vic says that the day before, they had met with the Blind Channel: "We had a lot of fun talking to them... we like their song a lot and we are so happy that there's another band bringing another side of rock music – that's really cool."

Among the performers, Måneskin do not go unnoticed: they play a genre unlike anyone else there, their rock is more glam and less introverted than the Finnish metalheads... So, they stand out for their originality together with the Go a (also appreciated by Måneskin who involve them in a live Instagram feed in which Damiano tries to learn their lyrics) and Barbara Pravi – to a lesser extent, also Victoria's and the Hooverphonic's performances are remarkable. In addition, Måneskin are beautiful, and the Etro suits, partially inspired by Bowie partially by Destiny's Child, as usual suits them well. During their performance, Ethan is extremely far from the rest of the band, on a sort of staircase where his shadow and his moving hair blend with the scenography, deliberately less over-the-top and more powerful than that of many of the others – especially most of the vocalists. The focus is on the music, not on the show, like at a Måneskin concert. What doesn't sound like a Måneskin concert is the fact that Damiano, given the Eurovision rule, is the only one actually live (Ethan plays, but the drums are not amplified – nor is bass and guitar). No inappropriate words either: this is what the regulation wants and, according to Vic, foreclosing the opportunity for a few words would be stupid. It's incredible how a very conservative Italian politician (Adinolfi) criticizes

Måneskin for 'bowing' to the rules. "The message of the song," Damiano tells *Il Fatto Quotidiano:*

> "It is neither contained in the word 'fuck' nor in 'balls'... it's a much broader thing, so changing those words doesn't change the meaning of the lyrics. I mean, if they had told us "change the song," "change the sounds," or "change the title," then it is clear that it would be about integrity and we should think about what we are going to bring. But here we have changed... two words."

Halfway through the vote, it seems that the two French speakers (Switzerland and France) are in the lead. When the representative of Macedonian TV expresses their vote, Italy is third. France takes the twelve points on the technical juries of many countries – when the Serbian technical jury declares their vote, France is first and they keep first place until the first recap. Only Slovenia, Croatia, Georgia, and Ukraine give their twelve points to Italy. Even Denmark, which Vic had claimed to represent in part, votes for Switzerland. Måneskin follow the voting together with their manager Marta Donà. When Croatia gives Italy their twelve points, Thomas screams as if he were at the stadium, but he seems the only one to believe in it. He also breaks a glass, immediately Damiano puts his head down to get rid of it.

The points from the technical jury for Italy are lacking, yet in the meantime – slowly but surely – those of the televoting rise up. When the Swedish jury is called upon, Italy is third after the two French-speaking singers. Only two countries haven't declared their technical jury vote yet. They are Switzerland and the Netherlands, neither of them votes for Italy. After every technical jury voted, Italy is fourth after

Malta, France, and Switzerland. Just like in Sanremo, it is the gap settled by televoting (as for Lithuania, Finland, Iceland, and Ukraine) that sends Måneskin to the top of the chart: they gained 318 points that lead the band right to the first position, overtaking Iceland and Ukraine. At that point, even Damiano ("I was dying of anxiety") begins to believe in it. When they film him, we can tell from his face that he didn't expect the result, while Vic starts screaming and hugging Marta Donà. Yet, the votes for Malta, Switzerland, and France haven't been declared. In Sanremo it takes less time to vote, less of the anxiety.

After the televote is communicated, Malta does not rise by much, France with Barbara Pravi does not pass Italy's 524 points. At that point of the race, Thomas Er Cobbra cries like a fountain hugging Vic, who later will say: "I was trembling with happiness and Thomas held me so tightly that I said to him: 'Easy, you are suffocating me'." Ethan keeps an eye on the billboard, his self-control is freezing him and Damiano is impatient. Switzerland, the great favorite of technical juries, does not reach the 250 points more they would need: Måneskin wins the Eurovision Song Contest. At that point Marta Donà also bursts into tears. Ethan, crying, stands for a few minutes, unable to move. He recovers after a while, hugging Damiano. The gap with France is remarkable, 524 points against 499, "and that's what counts the most for us," Vic will say at the press conference, "'cause that means that people are actually, like, enjoying our music." Jan Smit, The Dutch host, is keen to say that victory goes: "to the land of pizza and Sambuca" (it's rather unusual to be remembered for Sambuca but, yes, I guess we are). Before singing *Zitti e buoni* again, Måneskin need to calm down after the adrenaline rush. They do it by shouting: "Come on! Let's go!"

"We just want to say to the whole of Europe, to the whole world," says Damiano receiving the award, "rock and roll never dies!" In the live performance after their victory, the "touch your balls" (*toccarvi I coglioni*) are reinstated along with; "they don't know what the fuck they are saying" ("*non sa di che cazzo parla*") back into the lyrics. It doesn't matter anymore now.

Italy has won Eurovision three times: the first was in 1964 with the fourteen-year-old chaste and pure Gigliola Cinquetti singing *Non ho l'età* (*I'm not old enough* – to date a man). Then in 1990 another melodic singer who, touching on the hot topic of European Unity after the Berlin Wall, gained the award: it was Toto Cutugno and the song was *Together: 1992*.

Today, Gigliola Cinquetti is an intelligent woman who has little or nothing in common with that girl forced to embody a stereotype. On Måneskin, she praised the choice not to translate the lyrics in order to make Eurovision a place of plural linguistic beauty. Then she said:

> "Their music marks a change of pace, and I want to make a high-level comparison: in the Renaissance the classics were rediscovered and re-proposed by reinterpreting them in a modern way. They do the same with rock, which is in many ways the classical music of the twentieth century."

Even Toto Cutugno, who through Eurovision gained incredible popularity, especially in Eastern Europe, from Facebook said he was happy that, finally, he could pass the baton to Måneskin after thirty-one years.

"We feel like everything we've done since the day we met and the day we started playing on the street really makes sense and it's worth it," said Damiano at the press conference.

Despite the host of the Austrian jury who wished to: "infect the whole world with friendship and togetherness," an important French magazine – *Paris Match* – on May 23, accuses Damiano of having taken cocaine while waiting for the votes of the technical juries. The accusation is based on a fragment of the live show. No drugs are visible, only that Damiano keeps his head down. Yet, if you remember, Thomas, that was extremely nervous, had broken a glass and Damiano was trying to get rid of it.

It's kind of silly to think that someone would take drugs when the whole of Europe could see it. Perhaps those who accused him were just hoping to come up with a positive drug test, as rock stars are always associated with sex and drugs. Rockstars, but not Damiano, and it's funny that it was him under accusation, the same Damiano who, on many occasions, drew the media's attention to his self-discipline. The band had joked about this bias a few weeks earlier during the TV program *Una pezza di Lundini*, on Rai1. In fact, the first thing the singer asks after the accusations is to be subjected to a drug test; "because I wanted the gossip to stop as soon as possible." The test, for organizational reasons, is postponed to his return to Italy. Months later, interviewed by *LeHuffPost* in France, the front-man will say:

"When we first heard about it of course we were a bit upset because it's never, like, good to be accused of something like that – most of all if you never did something like that in your life. But after five minutes we realized that it was only rumors and it was pretty easy to shut it down, so we started celebrating again."

""You play rock music, you wear make-up, so you must do drugs," adds Vic, "No, it doesn't work like that."

Meanwhile, the social commentator, journalist and influencer Selvaggia Lucarelli writes on her social networks that the accusation is: "Incredible, because only an idiot could think that someone could start taking cocaine while the whole world is watching him," but it is also, "a serious matter because the victory of four young guys is besmirched by a slanderous lie, the journalist didn't even take the trouble to watch the offending video." Vasco Rossi, who in the past has actually had problems with cocaine, exclaims from Instagram, not without humor: "I am going to do the drug test too!" then he turns serious and says:

> "I find it ridiculous that the controversy came out of France that had the "maudit" poets. They never said anything about Lou Reed or the Rolling Stones and now they've come up with this cocaine thing. But on the one hand it's also nice that it happened because it shows how prejudices concerning rock die hard. And even if it was, what does it matter? You are there to evaluate the music, not the behaviors, the private life. Apart from the fact that it is clear that they are very clean. And fresh."

During the press conference after the victory – and after the bottle of champagne – a Swedish journalist asks Damiano a direct question: it is there that the front-man explains about the broken glass, adding: "I don't use drugs, please, guys, don't say that, no cocaine, please."

In fact, Barbara Pravi had performed a charming song that perfectly embodied an important side of the French musical identity. However, this does not justify the attempt of the press to sabotage Måneskin. "I know them well," declares Manuel Agnelli when asked, "they are really beyond clichés from the point of view of sex, drugs, and rock and roll. They are not boring at all, but they are not unstructured either – quite the contrary. This whole thing makes me laugh because the French are sore losers." I wouldn't really say so though; the talented French singer, after the competition, in the heat of the moment had declared that she was not at all disappointed because in any case, second place, "c'est la folie." Again, later she had expressed herself on the drug-controversy, leaving everything to the unquestionable judgment of televoting. "First of all, I don't care," she said:

> "It's not my business, I point out that they have been chosen by the public and the jury, so whether they take drugs or put their underwear on backward, it's not my problem."

Damiano's result is obviously cocaine-negative. France Télévision had already announced that they did not want to appeal. Barbara Pravi, who still triumphed for the technical jury, will again state her point of view from Instagram:

> "I see that there are controversies that are mounting without me, following the victory (very much deserved) of my Italian friends. So, I repeat here what I have already told the media: Måneskin were BRILLIANT on Saturday night, they were chosen by the viewers and therefore it is their place, their victory, their moment.

I am number two, very proud and very proud of this second place on the podium and therefore it would be nice if you didn't bring me up by attributing me words, intentions, or silences. *Vive l'Italie, vive la France*, long live rock and long live French *chanson*. Kisses, bisous, bravo and also long live underwear put on backward."

Months later, the *Los Angeles Times* will call the incident – thinking of classic rock: "Charmingly retro."
That evening, Eurovision have been seen by half of Europe and by part of Australia. After all, it is and it still remains the most-watched television show in the world. Many watchers, accustomed to pop-dance vocalists with over-the-top choreographies, were thrilled by *Zitti e buoni* and wanted to know more. May 2021 was when Måneskin were introduced to the world.

Only a few days after the end of the contest, on May 24, the band wrote on Facebook: "*Zitti e buoni* is #9 on the Spotify Global Chart. It's the most-streamed Italian song ever, something like this has never happened before." The band confirms that they will take part in two important German festivals: the Rock am Ring (in the Nürburgring of Formula 1, Germany) and the Rock Im Park in Nuremberg. Then there is the Tons of Rock in Oslo, where the headliners of their night are Faith No More (Iron Maiden and Deep Purple will follow in the next two days). On May 28, *Zitti e buoni* is the first Italian song in thirty years to enter the British chart at number 17. "No words can describe how happy and honored we are," states the band from Facebook, "Our music is spreading through more than thirty charts all over the world and this is literally insane." Official merchandising is released on May 31: it's all sold out in twenty-eight minutes. Pepsi chooses *Zitti e buoni* for the new advertising campaign. On June 20 *Zitti e Buoni* is awarded a gold record in Sweden. Again, in June, when they ask Damiano if he will sue *Paris Match*, the front-man replies to the magazine *Tv Sorrisi e Canzoni*:

"Filing a complaint? No, I won't because for me the issue has never even been opened. It was all just a big comic sketch, like Zelig [Italian comic TV show renamed after Allen's film]. If they apologize, I'm ready to accept it. But now we are only interested in celebrating, in spite of those who tried to hinder us."

The band has something else in mind. A proper international tour. And the United States.

Meanwhile, the relatives of the four Måneskin members take pictures with the two trophies: Eurovision (which stays at Damiano's for months) and Sanremo (which Er Cobbra steals at Vic's).

Part 7.

Las Vegas and the
American Dream

The meaning of art, in general, is just
something that you feel represented by.
(Ethan Torchio)

F rom this moment on, keeping up with Måneskin
becomes increasingly difficult: almost every day,
throughout the course of 2021, there is thrilling
news about them. New audiences, new stages, new TV shows
– some of those made history in United States broadcasting
– and old glories, ready for collaborations.

European gigs start between late May and early June. The
first unexpected novelty, however, is announced via social
media by Marta Donà on June 5, the band left her. "We spent
four unforgettable years together, full of dreams to be
fulfilled and of projects to accomplish," writes the now-
former manager on Twitter, "I brought you this far. From
now on, you have decided to go on without me. My heart is
broken, but I wish you the best in life, guys." It is rumored
that the hard choice was made for someone exceedingly high
up, even the name Simon Cowell is mentioned. When some
journalists ask Damiano, he replies that he hoped they would

pose him that question, for he was longing to deny it: the new manager is the old producer, Fabrizio Ferraguzzo, who created Exit Music Management just for them.

In June and July, the band alternate gigs between Continental Europe and Italy. Meanwhile, there's time to write and record a curious song written in two days, which almost seems like the international sequel to *I Wanna be Your Slave*. The title is *Mammamia*, the same as a well-known song by Abba, launched by Eurovision. It's easy to deduce what inspired it: the controversy over cocaine at Eurovision, and, at large, prejudices on sex, drugs, and rock and roll. Or the usual clichés about Italians, cool, sexy, and stylish; regardless of whom we're referring to ("why so hot? 'Cause I'm Italiano"). *Mammamia* represents Måneskin having fun with all this rubbish, writing a lyric that hints at *spitting* and *pissing* – a game, a mockery.

In mid-June, they are in Berlin, on the 18th, in Amsterdam, on the 20th, in Gothenburg where they shoot that crazy set inspired by *Mean Girls*, all in pink with Thomas and Damiano dressed as bunnies. On the 22nd, they are back in the now-familiar Copenhagen (where the band gets tattooed one more time). Now people recognize them, stop them, they are really famous, although they are not very aware of it yet. On June 24, they are in France and many are the fans waiting for them in front of their hotel. On the TV show *Quotidien*, the host touches on the cocaine issue by asking if they're still mad at France ("Nous en voulait pas à la France? Tout va bien entre nous?"). Måneskin are calm, peace is made and sealed by *LeHuffPost* France who make them listen to some French rock bands and artists. Their favorites are Téléphone, which Ethan already knows, and the Indochine, while Johnny Hallyday in *Allumer le feu* – a classic – is so defined by

Damiano: "He looks like Bono. Like a huge, aggressive Bono." Ethan makes a small gaffe when asked if any French artists have influenced Måneskin by citing Stromae, who is Belgian. Vic expands the gaffe by quoting Lous and the Yakuza, the whole band nods, but she's Belgian too. By now everything is fine between Måneskin and France, it will not be two small mistakes that will cause more diplomatic incidents.

LeHuffPost also asks if the band regrets doing Eurovision because of the drug controversy. "How should I regret it!?" Damiano replies, "it was free advertising, come on!"

After France, there is Poland. Unfortunately, a wave of homophobia is hitting the country, although homosexuality has been legal for longer there than England (1932 versus 1967). There are 'LGBT free' areas where those who identify with this acronym are denied services and hotels. There is no legal recognition for homosexual couples. What can a rock band do in this case? Raise their voice with a kiss. At the end of *I Wanna Be Your Slave*, Damiano kisses Thomas. Then he takes the microphone and shouts: "We think that everyone should be allowed to do this without any fear. We think that everyone should be completely free to be whoever the fuck they want. Thank you, Poland, LOVE IS NEVER WRONG."

Months later, when in Italy the law against homo-trans-phobia will not pass in Parliament, it is nice and coherent to see the demonstrators in Piazza della Repubblica, Florence, under a giant Gucci advertising sign representing the four Måneskin members as testimonials.

Meanwhile, the headline in the *New York Times* was: *They won Eurovision, can they conquer the world?*

On July 2, the four faces of Måneskin are up on *Times Square* – it's a Spotify commercial. Shortly after, on July 15, they release the video of *I Wanna Be Your Slave*. On Instagram, given the previous incident of Vic's naked breast being censored, the band writes: "please don't report us again for being hot." With this track – with the sexy spitting between Ethan and Vic, the apples of sin, a super ambiguous Damiano kissing Ethan and singing (playing on his surname) "maybe I am your David and you're my Goliah" – Måneskin try to force their launch on the US market. The title of the song – and the theme – recalls another; *I Wanna Be Your Dog* by Iggy Pop. For the Italian soundtrack of the film *Cruella*, between Sanremo and Eurovision, Måneskin had covered it.

Meanwhile, our international tour continues. It is still France where the magazine *Madmoizelle* interviews the band and Damiano confesses that he knows now how to better manage invasive fans. Then we move on to Switzerland, to a TV show playing the game: *Have you ever?* Where it turns out that the guys took part in the Black Lives Matter marches, and that Damiano can make tattoos on his own (they actually filmed him when he did the "Mammamia" tattoo on himself). The band begins to get appreciation from very famous people: Miley Cyrus, Franz Ferdinand, and Royal Blood. In the same summer, Italian sportspersons achieve excellent results by winning the men's European football championship against the hosts, the women's volleyball championship, the American football championship in Sweden against the hosts and by bringing home many medals in Tokyo. Not to mention science, Giorgio Parisi wins the Nobel Prize in physics.

In the meantime, Virginia Raggi mayor of Rome (not a relative of Thomas) in the council chamber of the municipality of Rome gives the band an official recognition: La Lupa Capitolina, the Capitoline She-Wolf. It's the symbol of Rome, the legend goes that Rome's founders – the twins Romolo and Remo – were raised and fed by a she-wolf. If, in the old days, old ladies of via del Corso called the police when Måneskin played under their windows, now at the heart of Rome's administration, people talk about those: "who have been lucky enough to hear them on the sidewalks of our town center." "Few artists are willing to welcome the world like the four Måneskin members," says Ernesto Assante on that occasion, the music critic compares the *Lupa* to the MBE recognition conferred on the Beatles by Queen Elizabeth. Victoria insists on a concept that she cares about: beyond the trends of the industry, Måneskin demonstrate that you can play rock today and be successful. "Also because," says Ethan, "if you believe in what you do, others will believe in it too." A super-gig will take place at the Circus Maximus in July of the following year, Rome had just recognized its children.

Meanwhile, on the other side of the Atlantic, their four faces appear again on Times Square.

Host Fabio Fazio celebrates the band, who chose to make his first TV appearance on his show, with an Instagram story in which he sings *Zitti e buoni* with his son in the car. Like Manuel Agnelli, Fazio also takes Måneskin's achievements personally.

This time, the one who turns the tables is none other than Iggy Pop.

The old Passenger decides to add his vocals to *I Wanna Be Your Slave*, in duet with Damiano. They release the song on August 6. The band meets him in a video-call and not in person, but the final result is still remarkable. It is remarkable how the glam seventies patina, already in the song, is enhanced by an iconic voice that lived through those years. But this is certainly not enough to convince some Italian critics of the value of Måneskin: in *Rolling Stone Italy,* Claudio Todesco again writes an article in which, on the one hand he mentions social-media-haters more ferocious than Iggy, and on the other, it is the author himself who resizes the value of this collaboration. According to him, having Iggy Pop singing one of Måneskin's songs is not that important for many reasons: the collaboration was at distance, at this moment Måneskin are stronger than Iggy on the market, Iggy himself lately (despite being called the 'pope' of rock by Todesco) has put his voice everywhere – and the journalist quotes duets with Kesha and Kylie Minogue. According to him – who once again seems to miss the staged aspect of glam rock and the honesty of certain Måneskin songs (like *Coraline*) – it makes more sense that someone over seventy is 'looking for redemption' than a twenty-year-old, and we really don't understand why. One may have already lived many lives at twenty-two. Moreover, it is not even clear why the 'filthy impulse' of *I Wanna Be Your Dog* is superior – and not just simply different – from *I Want to Be Your Slave* and its "sex as if it was a party." It is not clear either why Damiano's words at the Eurovision; "we don't do drugs, please don't say that," according to Todesco, would be indecent.

However, he verbalizes one thing correctly in this passage:

"Listening to *I Wanna Be Your Slave* with Iggy made me think that certain myths are more precious for those who adore them than for those who create them. It is rare for musicians to display the sectarianism typical of maniacal rock fans, who often harbor a sense of colossal superiority towards others and view certain collaborations as mutinies. They have some reason, of course, of cultural nature: that is, Måneskin does not come from rock as a subculture, but as a show... Iggy Pop singing with Måneskin upsets us, but for the American singer it was not a crazy idea: he has never been choosy. While in Italy there was a debate about whether Måneskin are rock or not, he came, threw us a head-bang and said: of course they are, you fools. Perhaps the search for exclusivity is just a slightly more evolved form of provincialism. Rock can also be this thing here, not three chords and the truth as Bono said, but three chords and one erection."

The article in *Rockol* is more relatable: Claudio Cabona, who wrote it, guesses that Iggy Pop did the feature to have fun after recognizing the hint to his song, and writes about how much all this is good for Italian music.

And here we are again following the band at the Ronquières Festival in Belgium, at the Open 'er again in Poland, then in Moscow, then again in Vienna, the "last page of this crazy summer tour," as the band writes on Facebook. In the meantime, however, while Måneskin are officially testimonials for Gucci, Spotify awards them as the most-streamed Italian artist ever and, as for the international charts, Maroon 5 are still on top – though in August, Måneskin almost reached them. Meanwhile, on TikTok, someone discovered the cover of *Beggin'* (staged back in

2017 on *X-Factor*). The band had already stored it in their memories. Yet, the song by Frankie Valli and the Four Seasons (the Jersey Boys of the musical) was slowly coming back from the past.

In the meantime, the Italian gigs of December 2021 are postponed to spring due to covid, but on the other hand they release the European dates of the Loud Kids Tour 2022 at the end of September: they include London, Berlin, Brussels, Paris and... they sell out in two hours. "When we put the tickets on sale," said Vic:

> "We were like, 'let's make a bet – How long till the tickets are gonna be sold out?' They asked me and I said 'maybe a week' and they were like 'oh, no, that's too short an amount of time.' And then one hour later... we read on Twitter 'I can't get my tickets' – we were like: 'what's going on?'"

The tickets were already gone, that's what was going on.

Mammamia is due to be released in October, the first performance will take place at the pre-listening party in Berlin. Spotify floods big cities, like New York and Toronto, with advertisements for the new song. On October the 19, they release the splatter video of the song: it begins with Vic driving a car and saying: "he is so fucking annoying," then she, Ethan, and Thomas dream about how to kill Damiano. Ethan, wearing a Union Jack vest that Geri Halliwell would have liked, sticks the front-man's head in the toilet and tries to drown him (behind, there's writing that says: "rest in piss"). Vic stabs him in the kitchen while she's making out with a girl (the writing this time is: "boys will be executed"). Thomas obviously kills him with – what else – a guitar. The result has something similar to Åkerlund's videos for Lady Gaga. The whole story, shot by Rei Nadal, ends with a strobe-splatter sequence for which the video has to put an epilepsy warning on YouTube. "Fun, but also tiring," said Vic, "'cause we shot only during the night, so we didn't sleep for three days." Damiano's "it's all about me" t-shirt is once again inspired by the film *Mean Girls*. He so wanted to give it an early aughts Lindsay Lohan feel.

On September 22, our folks are in London at the O2 Academy in Islington where they sing *I Wanna Be Your Dog* by Iggy Pop, Damiano takes Thomas Er Cobbra and his guitar on his shoulders. Meanwhile, the band is nominated as Best Group, Best Rock and Best Italian Act at the MTV European Music Awards.

Five days later, Måneskin make their triumphal entry into the United States.

The first to have them as guests is Jimmy Fallon on the *Tonight Show*. Jimmy Fallon does not interview them, they have two musical slots: the first for *Mammamia*, the second for *Beggin'*, which, despite being on the first EP from four years earlier, is now back to being a required single. One of the guests on the talk show is Drew Barrymore, who goes backstage to compliment the band and to take pictures with them, as a fan. On TikTok, she will call them: "The sexiest band on the planet."

That same evening, Måneskin play at the Bowery Ballroom. It's their first concert in the US, "one of the wildest gigs we've ever played." Thomas will remember that night's outfit as one of his favorites, the retro style made him look a bit like his idol Jimmy Page. Vic and Ethan will consider it the best concert they ever did, the one where everything went the right way. The venue is small (there are about 600 seats), but it's considered one of the best in the United States and Patti Smith is a regular. Some Italians write on Facebook that those present at the gig must be "all Italians," but in fact, the public is mixed, given the hype of recent months and the success of *Mammamia* and *Beggin',* which will soon go platinum. Singer Little Steven takes a selfie with the band and writes on his social media that Måneskin are: "bringing rock back to the mainstream world." A *Reddit* user, called Bella, tells us about that evening from her perspective: the girls who competed to grab Damiano during crowd-surfing, a plastic cup, possibly, thrown on the singer's head (it was actually Rolling Stones merchandising panties), Damiano drinking a lot of water and then spitting while singing, a very excited audience. The same user claims to have "post-concert depression" while writing. For the autograph signing at the end of the concert two hours later, security had to line people up inside metal barriers.

No, they weren't all Italians in the audience – It's Italian people who often underestimate their artists.

In New York, Måneskin are interviewed by *Z100 New York*, which broadcasts from the tip of the Empire State Building. To the hosts, Maxwell and Stal Rosas, the band confess that this is their first time in the Big Apple for almost everyone. Damiano has been there before, but he was too little to remember. Vic adds that they haven't seen much due to the jet lag that has left them a little sleepy. Meanwhile, an article by ANSA defines them as: 'The Italian Fab Four.'

At this point, the news about Måneskin opening for the Stones at the Allegiant Stadium in Las Vegas on November the 6, has already spread. Mick and Keith personally chose them. And if they are a rock band to Mick and Keith, their judgment is final.

But first things first. The band is nominated for the American Music Awards as Favorite Trending Song, the AMA are on November 21. Måneskin then go to LA, it's the beginning of November.

I am sure everybody knows that Los Angeles is one of the iconic cities of rock, a city that the whole band (but Thomas in particular, as a huge fan of Guns N' Roses and Red Hot Chili Peppers) dreams about. They managed to get there, not without a little suspense, as Ethan falls ill in New York before leaving. Luckily enough, it's not covid but only flu. So, they confirmed the gig: on November 1, Måneskin perform at the Roxy Theater, a famous venue on the Sunset Strip where irrelevant names have played, such as Frank Zappa, Bob Marley, Guns N' Roses, Nirvana, David Bowie, Dire Straits... In short, if we list together those I have mentioned, we only get the history of rock!

The gig gets sold out and everyone – not just Thomas – is excited. Vic declared to the *Los Angeles Times* that she absolutely wants to see the Rainbow Bar among the other venues, "I grew up on metal and glam rock, so we were all sitting on the couch in there, like, 'This is where Lemmy and Mötley Crüe used to hang out'." Instead Damiano declares that playing at the Roxy; "makes you realize that you're actually doing something great. Something cool. So, it's a good feeling." The first gig he ever saw was that of Guns N' Roses.

The gig goes very well. US fans had time to listen to the Italian songs as well as *Beggin'* and *Mammamia*. "We were playing songs in Italian from the record that we didn't think were very known here," Vic will say after the concert to the

Los Angeles Times, "But everyone knew the words, even if it was harder for them to sing."

In LA, the band begins the promotional tour of radios and TV shows. The day after the gig, they are guests at HITS1 LA, Thomas feels like a kid in a candy store. When asked how the gig had gone, he answers: "It was incredible... It was really emotional for us: a lot of people in front of us, without barriers so... The crowd was pretty hot." The two hosts point out that there was a massive queue outside the venue on Sunset. That is, we are in Los Angeles, in an iconic venue, and four Italians under the age of twenty-five are fully booked. "It feels surreal," replies Damiano. Host Tony Fly, of Italian descendent, defines them as: "part of the rebirth of rock and roll," and asks if they have realized how big they have become. "Every day we understand new parts of what's happening," Damiano replies, "actually, after the Eurovision, we saw this bomb blowing up... it's hard to realize, but we just stay with the vibe and try to enjoy it." As for the EMA nominations, the band exclaims almost in sync: "it's insane!" When asked: "What makes you different from other bands?" The singer replies confidently: "We are not drug-addicted." "Can you eat cacio e pepe (cheese and black pepper pasta) in peace in Rome?" host Symon asks, "No, we make it ourselves," Damiano replies again.

Speaking of food, during the same day on a radio show on SIRIUSXM, the three hosts – Nicole Ryan, Stanley T. and Ryan Sampson – play the game of "see if we pronounce Italian words right" with the four Måneskin members. This is how they sounded for them: "Recoda" (ricotta), "pepperdele" (pappardelle, rolling the r), "penecchon" (panettone – this makes Damiano laugh a lot), the classic "pasta fajoul" (pasta and beans, fagioli), "ribollida" (ribollita). The best at pronouncing Italian names is Stanley T. who gets the word "calamari" (squid) right on the first try.

TikTok will then retransmit the Roxy gig on November 13.

On November the 3, Måneskin are at the Gucci Love Parade, which is also in Los Angeles. The House of Gucci, of which they are testimonials, presents the new collection. At the party, they put on *Beggin'* and Damiano, in white, sings with the record. The band then finally got a chance to have a close encounter with a superstar who has been following them for a while: Miley Cyrus. In the crowd, there are also Gwyneth Paltrow and Diane Keaton.

On how it happened that they become the Rolling Stones opening act, Damiano told HITS1 LA: "We just got the news, 'Do you want to open for the Rolling Stones?' 'Oh no, I am busy'." On November 2, the band had not yet exchanged a single word with Mick Jagger. However, it is Joel Madden from Good Charlotte who had a long chat with them about playing the music genre they prefer and how hard it was to emerge with rock in Italy. The Good Charlotte singer, coming from a troubled family and raised in an environment hostile towards creativity, draws a (sadly) universal moral from the Måneskin's story:

> "Around the world, there are tons of places where people don't believe in art. If you can't create, if you can't be yourself, if you can't live the truth of who you are, then you're being oppressed in some way. I think every artist has felt that way... So, I think the four of you together, you're telling this story that needs to be told but from the

perspective of kids who grew up in Italy who were basically told, "There's no point in doing this. There's no point in being yourself"".

November 6, finally comes. The name of the band lights up at the Allegiant Stadium in Las Vegas. The four Måneskin members are dressed in the colors of the US flag. To emphasize the no-gender style, Thomas wears a bra. They open the concert with a song in Italian – *Nel nome del padre.* Ethan, the former "terrible drummer" waving his super-straight hair, hits the drums hard. Thomas seems to come from another era, he even does *that thing,* playing his guitar with his teeth. Vic stands out for her way of playing, striding across the stage, and – well – because she's a woman and her peers consider her an equal.

Before the second song, Damiano wants to say that:

> "This is our first stadium, it's a pleasure and it's an honor for us to be here and have the chance to warm you up before we get on stage with one of the greatest bands of all time. So, thank you for this chance, we're gonna give you 100%. Have fun."

The first stadium opening up for the Rolling Stones is not for everybody.

The band keeps playing: first *Zitti e Buoni*, then *Take me out* by Franz Ferdinand mixed with *Somebody Told Me* from the Killers. Then comes *Beggin'*. Who would have thought that the old routine from *X-Factor* would prove so useful someday? Not even Manuel Agnelli, that's for sure. The song that follows is *Coraline* and the intensity is palpable. After comes the most Brit of the pieces, *For your love*. Then: *I*

Wanna Be Your Dog again, that Damiano dedicates to Iggy Pop and *I Wanna Be Your Slave*.

After forty minutes of the gig, the band leaves the stage to the Rolling Stones. They have plenty of time to take a shower, change their clothes and enjoy the headliners as the Stones come out about an hour later. First, there is a small photographic tribute to Charlie Watts, who recently passed away. He was a quiet drummer, like Ethan.

As we know, Mick Jagger later thanked Måneskin in Italian. Italian magazines wrote a lot about that.

And this was their night on top of the rock world, perhaps one of the most surreal evenings of the Måneskin dream.

After the Rolling Stones, *Variety* dedicates a page to the band from Rome. The title is emblematic: *The Italian Band That Defied the Odds and Brought Rock Back to the US*. The breath of fresh air, which, however many in Italy had perceived before, reaches as far as the West Coast.

The important opening was with the Rolling Stones, but it is impossible not to think of the Beatles who, by invading the United States, gave new life to rock and roll. Journalist Jessica Shalvoy defines Måneskin's path as "far from ordinary" then quotes an anecdote by Victoria about the Stones: "I saw them when they played at Circo Massimo (Circus Maximus) in Rome. I didn't have tickets, so I just went there and tried to sneak in through the barriers. It didn't really work, but I saw a couple of songs!" The journalist comments: "Going from teenage trespasser to opening act is but one of many full-circle moments these young artists will experience." "Each member of Måneskin," Shalvoy remarks, "is nothing less than captivating on stage." As for the songs in Italian, "The language barrier was practically non-existent, with zero effect on the crowd, who went crazy for *Zitti e Buoni*, the song that won them Eurovision earlier this year."

The funniest thing about Måneskin's US success is perhaps this unexpected return of *Beggin'* via TikTok, not at all stimulated by the band. Victoria comments on that as follows:

> "More and more we think that the cool thing about TikTok is that if people like a song, it becomes viral and it's very natural. It's not like it used to be in the past where for a song to become famous, it had to go on the radio. Here people can make their own choice."

The journalist then remembers how many times the band heard the sentence: "you won't make it because rock doesn't sell," between Italy and Europe: *X-Factor*, Sanremo, Eurovision. "We never had the goal of winning," says Damiano, "but the fact that everyone was telling us it's impossible to win just got us more fueled."

Around that time, on JoJo Wright's microphones, the band confirms that since their victory at Eurovision in May they have had about five days off. It's the same interview in which Vic says that many young people, after their success, have started to: "grab instruments and start bands, this is very cool." Damiano then confesses that: "I am trendy in the milf zone," and tells a few stories about horny fans: one who grabbed "my package" during an autograph signing in front of hundreds of people (something similar happened to Manuel Agnelli during stage-diving), and one that he found in front of his room at three in the morning in Russia, that he did not let in. This last episode confirms that Måneskin redefine rock and roll lifestyle standards.

November keeps going, Måneskin are guests on the Ellen Show. Meanwhile, they release the vinyl edition of *Mammamia*. At the Europe Music Awards in Budapest, the award for best Italian artist goes to Aka7ven, yet Måneskin win the Best Rock award. Other candidates were Coldplay, The Foo Fighters, The Killers, Kings of Leon, and Imagine Dragons. It is another incredible achievement.

As we've briefly mentioned before, in Italy a law against homo-trans-phobia, that is, the Decree of Law so named as the Member of Parliament Honorable Alessandro Zan (DDL Zan), wasn't approved, though the majority of Italians wanted it. Alluding to that, accepting the award, Damiano says:

> "This year, in particular, we must be proud of our country for the results achieved not only by us but by many sportsmen and by many cultural personalities. Too bad for civil rights, where we continue to lag behind and instead, it would have been the most important victory for us."

One of the conservative politicians who celebrated when the law did not pass (Simone Pillon), takes the ball to criticize the makeup, the transparencies, and the garter belts that Måneskin wore at the EMA. "Considering the culottes and the garters, we will soon get to men's bras," writes the senator (and the note keeps going with anti-abortion speeches). He didn't pay enough attention, since Thomas had worn a men's bra during the Stones concert.

The senator then adds as follows:

"Obviously, once they have taken the microphone, they cannot avoid whining about the resounding rejection of #ddlZan. Looking at them, I wonder: where would the discrimination be? It is easy to follow the stream of the politically corrupted. As young people who claim they are alternative and rebellious, I would have expected something different, I don't know, the boys in tuxedos and the young lady in an evening dress on stage, complete with statements such as: "children have the right to have a Mom and a Dad." Then, yes, we would have seen something truly disruptive. Sure, they would have forgotten about the mainstream awards and cheers, but they would have proven to be truly out of the box. Instead, it is always the same old story."

Time will pass on the senator's words. Yet, Damiano promptly replies – and thank goodness he does that jokingly: "You're right Simo, next time Tuxedos and paPillon" (we call a Bow tie by the French name, "papillon," and remember the senator's surname is Pillon). The "next time" in this case, is the American Music Awards: during the ceremony, Måneskin actually dress in tuxedos and bow ties like the Four Seasons – even Vic, no one puts the "young lady" in an evening dress if she doesn't want to. Honorable Pillon promptly replies: "This time I can't help but congratulate Måneskin. Great outfits guys! And congratulations on keeping your promise. I'll have to hum *Beggin'* in the Senate to make it up to you." And the story ends with this image.

Beggin' does not win the AMA for Favorite Trending Song, that goes instead to *Body* by Meghan Three Stallion. US fans, perhaps underestimated by the marketing department, would like to hear something different of Måneskin's repertoire. "I love *Beggin'*, I do," writes a user on Facebook, "but I wish they would play other songs during the big live performances." Months later Lisa Worden, director of programing at iHeartMedia, will say: "It's important to give them a chance to be more than a single. They deserve to have more of their music exposed. I saw them at the Roxy and they're a force. I think people will walk away with a new respect for them."

On November 23, Måneskin have no nominations at the Grammys, but they read those of the classical music records. Damiano tries hard to pronounce each name in his part in their language of origin. Vic is in Rome, this creates a bit of confusion among the fans but, in times of covid, it happens.

On November 29, the band plays *Beggin'* and *Mammamia* at *The Voice* US. Then, it's time to fly back home. "Home" as in X-Factor Italia.

Four years later, Måneskin are back as guests along with Coldplay on the TV show that launched them. They open with *Beggin'* and continue with *I Wanna Be Your Slave*, *Zitti e Buoni* and *Mammamia,* right on the stage of the Assago Forum where they gained second place in 2017. Now they come back in triumph. At the end of the Sanremo song, Damiano walks towards the judges' table: there are Mika, the trapper Hell Raton, the singer Emma Marrone and once again proud mentor Manuel Agnelli. In front of them, Damiano goes stage-diving, covering his lower parts against invasive fans. The studio explodes.

Chris Martin will later tell RTL radio that he met Måneskin on the show. "We love them," says the Coldplay singer, "in fact, we were going to play a bit of their song today on *X-Factor*, but then we realized that they were playing as well."

Meanwhile, on Facebook the band publishes a picture from 2017, and one of the evenings before, the caption goes: "Thank you *X-Factor* Italy for having welcomed us once again on a stage that is so important to us, it was magical."

In Russia, VKontakte, the most popular social network, appoints Måneskin as: "Foreign Artist of the Year." *Teatro d'ira vol. 1* reaches one billion Spotify streams and the band is nominated twice at the BRIT Awards, for "Best International Group" and "Best International Song." Four cute pictures of Thomas, Vic, Ethan, and Damiano (the latter with a cigarette in his mouth) as children are posted on Facebook by the end of the year. The caption reads: "These 4 kids made it to the end of 2021" – it was fruitful, it was crazy, but surely it wasn't easy.

Meanwhile, below the video of *Beggin'* as performed at the Streamy Awards, Luca Ward, the Italian voice of Russell Crowe, writes: "gladiators of rock."

In Pianoro, near Bologna, in October a fire broke out at a feline shelter. Unfortunately, eight cats died. Damiano and his partner Giorgia, who live with two cats (Lego and Bidè), wanted to give them a remarkable Christmas present: a nice donation. "We just saw what happened," Damiano writes:

> "My partner and I immediately decided to help you. We own two cats ourselves and cannot imagine the suffering you have been through. It was the least we could do, and we would love to come and see you at the shelter."

These are words that every cat person could subscribe to, everyone who helped Pianoro. Yet, those words are even more pleasing when they come from an international superstar who has spent his last few months elsewhere, from "a young boy with a noble and sensitive soul," they write from the feline shelter, "which, among thousands of commitments, has been able to find the time and the way to be close to us. He moved us a lot."

From Instagram, Damiano wishes a Merry Christmas 2021, while holding Lego in his arms. He's naked, of course.
On December 31, our fellows are playing on the West Coast at Dick Clark's New Year's Rockin' Eve. The *Los Angeles Times* writes about them: "Måneskin is an almost unnervingly lithe band of twenty-somethings who can squeeze into seventies David Bowie bodysuits." The title of the article is "How four seventies-obsessed Italians became America's favorite new rock band" and judging by the various "I am learning Italian because of you" on Facebook, it must be true. "The fact that there's a band in the top of the charts playing just three instruments; it's something that hasn't happened for so long," says Vic to *The Los Angeles Times:* "But we didn't expect it to happen in such a short amount of time." On January 22, the band is a guest at the legendary SNL show.

Lisa Worden from iHeartMedia wanted Måneskin at their ALTer EGO rock festival in Los Angeles. Well, she got them. The band played *Zitti e Buoni, Mammamia, Beggin', For Your Love* and *I Wanna Be Your Slave*. The US audience now knows them well, according to Worden, they know them better than Frankie Valli and the old authors of *Beggin':* "I bet a good portion of my audience didn't even realize it was a Four Seasons cover," she says.

The whole crucial phase of Måneskin's career took place during the covid period, which led to changes and cancellations of gigs. In mid-January therefore, the band through Damiano's voice, is forced to issue a statement announcing that the European Tour in the arenas (indoors) must be postponed due to the different anti-covid regulations of the various countries. The new dates will be released in March. Meanwhile, however, the band also announces another homecoming: the band is back at Sanremo, as special guests.

"Sanremo is home," they state at the press conference:

> "We arrived a year ago without any expectations, but from that moment on everything changed suddenly. A year has passed, we have traveled around the world, and we are here again to celebrate everything that has happened to us. And we want to celebrate on the same stage, together with the Sanremo audience and with Amadeus, who first believed in us. Without him, all this would not have happened."

The newspaper *La Repubblica*, who calls them: 'the four of Monteverde,' then remembers the list of surreal things that happened to Måneskin after Sanremo: the achievements, but also "Ed Sheeran's advice over a beer, lunch with Chris Martin, an evening with Beck around Los Angeles..." In 2022, the audiences of Coachella, Rock in Rio, Rock am Ring, Lollapalooza, Reading & Leeds await them. Then Rome will follow, at the Circus Maximus, "at home in a beautiful place, the most beautiful in the world."

The first show of Sanremo, again with Amadeus as the host and artistic director, is on February 1, 2022. Amadeus himself leads them (recklessly driving a golf cart) through the streets of the town that's on the coast, so Vic asks from behind: "Shall we go to the sea?" No, we shan't. Let's go on the Ariston Theater stage instead and play *Zitti e Buoni* once again.

Yet, Måneskin don't like giving the audience what they expect. When we spoke about the disc *Teatro d'Ira*, we left *Coraline* behind. It is a poignant ballad which the band presented on Facebook like this:

"It's our fairy tale, the story of a little girl who does not find her place in the world because she is too pure and fragile. Through a sweet melody, the song retraces a path that gradually becomes more and more distressing and that seems to be hopeless. Instead, the song wants to give it a little hope."

Many of the reviewers thought that the protagonist of the song was an abused child.

On the evening of February 1, the second song that the band plays is *Coraline*, supported by the Sanremo orchestra that had already embellished *Zitti e Buoni* the year before. The performance is incredibly intense, so much so that Damiano starts to cry in the middle of the song. His voice remains steady, but his eye makeup fades a little. Sanremo, and perhaps half of Italy, did not expect that from Måneskin. The Ariston Theater explodes into a loud hand-stripping applause and a standing ovation. The audience shouts "Måneskin!" Amadeus spontaneously hugs Damiano, who tries to hold his tears back. Yes, something at Ariston has changed. The days of the audience booing Placebo are gone.

"Damiano David's tears at the end of Måneskin's performance on the stage of Sanremo," writes *Cosmopolitan* Italia, "have impressed everyone since the leader of the band, of 'Mammamia', has never appeared more fragile, more moved and more emotional than this." Damiano himself will provide the key, the reason for his emotional performance, with a post on Instagram.

> "Thanks to all of you who have understood the meaning and importance of this song in my life. Thanks to my mates who took it to the stage with me. Thanks to Fabrizio Ferraguzzo who produced it and today he is our support, our best friend and our manager. Thanks to Amadeus, who gave me the opportunity to take it to the most important stage in Italy. And thanks to you Giorgia, who made me write and live it. To all of you, and to the music, simply thank you."

Giorgia Soleri has been Damiano's partner for five years now, despite rumors (groundless rumors) that foresaw a breakup in January 2022. On the evening of February 1, she was in the front row at the Ariston Theatre. By trade, Giorgia is a model, she is very popular on Instagram. Yet, it was after Damiano's post that many noticed that she has the word "Coraline" tattooed on her arm. Is she the protagonist of the song?

Surely, life for Giorgia in the last two years has not been easy: after years of painful menstruation, and doctors who told her that she had no illnesses, making her feel like a fool, the diagnosis came: endometriosis and vulvodynia. Vulvodynia: "affects the area of the vulva, where small nerve endings begin to grow in a disordered manner which causes rather acute pain, irritation, burning, and redness," they write in *Cosmo*. One in seven women in Italy suffers from it. Endometriosis, on the other hand, due to a mucous membrane that adheres where it should not, brings severe pain during menstruation, in sexual intercourse and during defecation. Even the salty seawater in Greece hurt Giorgia. In addition to blood in the urine and stool, there is also weakness and depression.

Although these are two terrible diseases, maybe the worst thing (for Giorgia and for everybody else) was the delay in the diagnosis. It takes five years on average to diagnose vulvodynia, seven and a half for endometriosis – It took eleven years for Giorgia. It's horrible when doctors downplay a debilitating disease, Giorgia was also told that the pain was in her head and that she was frigid, "solve your fear of penises." Reading about her rigmarole and those of other women, I couldn't help but think about comedienne Gilda Radner. Those who are familiar with her story will remember how a year of: "she has nothing, she is just stressed," had persuaded the actress that she was just neurotic. Instead, she had uterine cancer.

The uterus, that's it! It must be that which causes all the issues, for its pathologies are underestimated on the same old stupid cultural bias of the hysterical woman. That's why Giorgia is a feminist and gives a voice to all those women who are less exposed to the media, dealing with the same illnesses. The Italian Ministry of Health does not consider them as such, the public health care department does not cover them, and there are few experts who recognize them. Despite everything, Giorgia shares her partner's philosophy when she says that a country begins to be for young people when young people take it. The same goes for women. While Måneskin won Eurovision, Giorgia was invited to

Parliament. "I even went so far as to take painkiller injections," she said, "I spent whole days in bed, bleeding, crying, urinating." The Honorable Lucia Scanu presented a bill in Parliament to make those illnesses recognized by the National Health Service and to make treatment and diagnosis accessible to all patients as, once the diagnosis is made, the treatments is expensive. After the operation, Giorgia pays 300 euros for physiotherapy rehabilitation, then there are the gynecologist and the psychologist. "I spend 600 euros a month," wrote the model on social media, "if I weren't privileged, I couldn't do it." That's a lot of money. And politics takes a long time, so in October the feminist collective *Non una di meno* (*Not one less*) has called a large demonstration to press on the subject. Giorgia was in the front row, Damiano was with her.

So back to the question. Is Giorgia the *Coraline* of the song, the girl who cries and suffers anxiety? Of course, if she were Damiano provides a masculine insight that shows he really is a nice guy. That said, as the journalist Selvaggia Lucarelli recalls, after a conference on vulvodynia in which Giorgia and Damiano participated together in February 2022, beware of toxic narratives: Giorgia is not to be defined only for her illness and Damiano is not a hero – he just does what everyone in love should do. Vulvodynia has also been defined as a 'marriage-breaking disease' and it is in this ugly expression that stands the opposite of love and support on which Giorgia can count. The traditional education would want a man to leave a woman who is not performing, sexually-wise. It's the same type of education that makes certain doctors say: "solve your fear of penises," to weak and depressed women whose pain is absolutely real.

At that conference on vulvodynia, among other things, the famous bill was also presented and Giorgia, by activism, gave her decisive contribution to it. While I am writing, the news came through that the regional administration of Latium (that's where Rome is) recognized vulvodynia as a chronicle, debilitating disease. As the National Health Service is managed on a regional scale in Italy, it's a tiny yet crucial step forward.

Part 8.

Epilogue

T he Brit Awards have just passed. Måneskin didn't get any awards (neither did ABBA, as a matter of fact) but they were there. It was quite impossible, when the band awarded Wolf Alice as "Best Group," not to notice Vic's latex, Thomas's fetish laces and Damiano's choker, with a sex toy hanging on it. All by Gucci, of course. Aside from the nice details on the clothing, that has been an excellent opportunity to party with good old Ed Sheeran, described as a 'party animal,' winner of the "Songwriter of the Year" award.

Meanwhile, when Damiano went to the stadium to see his beloved Rome, some paparazzi caught Thomas with his girlfriend Lavinia Albrizio. Eurovision this year will take place in Turin, the hosts will be Alessandro Cattelan, Mika, and Ethan's old crush, Laura Pausini. The drummer in the meantime got engaged to another Laura (Alfonsa Castelli) who lives in Berlin. Vic's private life is quite mysterious, as she is openly bisexual, some paparazzi claimed to have taken a picture of her with her girlfriend. Who knows...?

Like any rock band, Måneskin's story is full of crazy moments. The accusation from Italian melodic band Cugini di Campagna for copying their look. Parodies from fans on Instagram stories, some very funny like *Ethan the tired mom friend*, where the funny moments in which the drummer acts like a mother towards the bandmates are collected. The compilations of stories from Vic having fun with Instagram's filters. Damiano's awkward stories of shameless women who touch him, lick him in the face and chase him without consent, up to hotel rooms.

Our story ends here, in February 2022. Yet, the future of music is right around the corner. Måneskin will take good care of it.

Small dictionary
of Italian personalities

- **Amadeus (Amedeo Umberto Rita Sebastiani):** former DJ and TV host. Artistic director and host of Sanremo in the years 2020, 2021 and 2022.

- **Ernesto Assante:** important music critic and Roman university teacher.

- **Luca Barbarossa:** singer-songwriter (he won the Sanremo Festival in 1992) and host of the radio show Radio Due Social Club together with Andrea Perroni.

- **Franco Battiato:** important Italian songwriter. He started out playing electro-experimental music in the seventies, he turned to sophisticated pop in the eighties. He's popular for his esoteric interests and his intellectual lyrics, often quoting far away Oriental places.

- **Orietta Berti:** folk-melodic singer, she started in 1961. When she was young, the press dubbed her "the nightingale of Cavriago," that's her town. Much loved by all age groups, she recently collaborated with Fedez and the glam performer Achille Lauro on the summer hit *Mille* (*One thousand*).

- **Giovanna Botteri:** journalist, specialized in politics. Her mother was a Montenegrin. She covered the Balkan conflict and, for a long time, she has been a foreign correspondent from New York for Tg1. In 2020, she covered the first wave of the covid-19 pandemics.

- **Michele Bravi:** young singer-songwriter, winner of the seventh edition of X Factor.

- **Caparezza (Michele Salvemini):** his street name literally means Curly Head, he is an Apulian rapper. His genre is conscious/alternative hip hop. He is well-known for his cartoon-like voice and his ferociously ironic lyrics.

- **Alessandro Cattelan:** former VJ and TV host. He hosted X-Factor Italia from 2011 to 2020. Together with Laura Pausini and Mika, he will host Eurovision 2022.

- **CCCP:** punk rock band active from 1982 to 1990, they disbanded on the day of the German reunification. If you like Italian underground music, you can't miss them.

- **Adriano Celentano:** world-famous, iconic Italian singer and actor, born in 1938.

- **Gigliola Cinquetti:** singer and writer. She started at fourteen, her stage persona was famous for being chaste and pure. She won the Copenhagen Eurofestival edition of 1964.

- **Colapesce (Lorenzo Urciullo) and Di Martino:** duo of songwriters with solo projects on their own. Their *Musica Leggerissima* made a splash at Sanremo 2021.

- **Carmen Consoli:** Sicilian singer-songwriter and multi-instrumentalist.
- **Toto Cutugno:** world-famous Italian melodic singer-songwriter, he won Eurovision in 1992, Zagreb edition. His most famous song is *L'Italiano,* that has a curious cover in Hindi, part of the soundtrack of the Bollywood film *Mann.*

- **Fabrizio De André:** he is considered the greatest among Italian songwriters. He grew up in Genoa, like many songwriters of the sixties. It was Mina's version of his *La canzone di Marinella* (*Marinella's song*) that made him decide to choose music as a career. Friend of Luigi Tenco, he was one of the two popular singers to go to his funeral.

• **Diodato:** melodic singer-songwriter, winner of the Sanremo Festival 2020 and former partner of Levante.

• **Lucio Fabbri:** musician, arranger, multi-instrumentalist. He was in PFM from 1979 to 1987. He was the musical director of *X-Factor Italia* from 2008 to 2019, later he was hired as an arranger for *Italia's got Talent* from 2015. In 2011, he played with the Blues Brothers Band.

• **Fabio Fazio:** TV host. He hosted Sanremo in 1999, 2000 (with Luciano Pavarotti), 2013 and 2014. Since 2003, he hosts the talk show *Che tempo che fa?* (*What's the weather like?*) co-hosted by comedienne Luciana Littizzetto.

• **Fedez:** street name of Federico Lucia, rapper. He has been a judge on *X-Factor* from 2014 to 2018. Since 2018, he has been married to Chiara Ferragni. They have a son and a daughter.

• **Chiara Ferragni:** thanks to her familiarity with Instagram, she firstly became a blogger then an influencer, then a fashion entrepreneur. She is considered a self-taught social media marketing expert. Since 2018, she has been married to Fedez. They have a son and a daughter.

• **Rosario Fiorello:** he is a showman, a radio speaker and a singer. He started with a Karaoke show in the nineties and for many years he hosted the radio show *W Radio 2*. For two years he hosted the radio show *Il Rosario della Sera (The Evening Rosary)* where Måneskin went twice as guests.

• **Drusilla Foer (Gianluca Gori):** more than an *en travesti* character, she is the veritable alter-ego of actor Gianluca Gori. She is a TV host, a writer (her autobiographical book is called: "You don't know what shame is"), and a singer. She presents herself as very cultivated and full of humor.

• **Frankie Hi-nrg (Francesco di Gesù):** he is the first conscious rapper to have gained success in Italy with the song *Quelli che benpensano* in 1997.

• **Ghemon (Giovanni Luca Picariello):** rapper, songwriter and former graffiti artist.

• **Hell Raton (Manuel Zappadu):** Italian-Ecuadorian rapper and producer, part of the Machete Crew. He collaborated with Orietta Berti in the single *Luna Piena*. He was a judge on X Factor in 2020 and 2021.

• **Jovanotti (Lorenzo Cherubini):** singer-songwriter and former DJ, he was the first to bring rap to popularity in Italy (even if very contaminated with funky and pop).

• **Levante (Claudia Lagona):** writer and songwriter, her first hit was in 2013 with the song Alfonso. Her genre is indie-pop. Ex-wife of Simone Cogo from the Bloody Beetroots and former girlfriend of Diodato.

• **Luciana Littizzetto:** comedienne characterized for a shameless and sassy style. During Sanremo 2003, she kissed the host Pippo Baudo for provocation. She has been collaborating with Fabio Fazio since 2005.

• **Selvaggia Lucarelli:** former theater actress, famous social reporter, blogger, and influencer.

• **Gabriele Mainetti:** director and author, together with screenwriter Nicola Guaglianone, of films *Lo chiamavano jeeg robot* (*They called him Jeeg Robot*) And *Freaks Out*.

• **Mara Maionchi:** record company employee and talent scout since 1968, X-Factor judge from 2008 to 2010 and from 2017 to 2019.

• **Alessia Marcuzzi:** showgirl, actress and TV host. In the movie *Il mio west* (*My west*) David Bowie kills her.

• **Marlene Kuntz (Cristiano Godano):** alternative rock band, active since 1987, the front-man is Cristiano Godano. They teamed up with Skin from Skunk Anansie for *La canzone che scrivo per te* (*The Song I write for you*).

• **Emma Marrone:** singer. She started her career from the reality show *Amici* (*Friends*). She won Sanremo in 2012. She participated in Sanremo 2022 with Francesca Michielin as conductor.

• **Enrico Melozzi:** is a conductor and producer, Fellow of London College. During six editions, he conducted the orchestra for various singers in Sanremo.

• **Ermal Meta:** Italo-Albanian singer-songwriter who started in the band *La Fame di Camilla*. He won Sanremo in 2018 teaming up with the singer-songwriter Fabrizio Moro.

• **Francesca Michielin:** singer-songwriter, she won X-Factor 2011. She ended up second in Sanremo 2016 and, given the renouncement of the winners, she took part in ESC, positioning herself as sixteenth. A longtime collaborator of Fedez, they ranked in second place at Sanremo 2021.

- **Mina (Anna Mazzini):** also known as "the tiger of Cremona." She is one of the most important singers and vocalists of Italy, active since 1958. Her version of *La Canzone di Marinella* (*Marinella's Song*) launched Fabrizio De André. She has been retired from the scene since 1978, yet she kept making records. She lives between the town of Brescia and Switzerland. She participated in Sanremo for the last time in 1961, swearing not to set foot there again.

- **Vincenzo Mollica:** important journalist, expert of cinema and music. He currently has Parkinson's disease.

- **Gianni Morandi:** Italian singer, active since 1962. Lately, he is also a star of Facebook. He won Sanremo in 1987 teaming with Enrico Ruggeri and Umberto Tozzi.

- **Negramaro:** Apulian pop band, named after a wine.

- **Enrico Nigiotti:** singer-songwriter from Livorno, after X-Factor he took part in Sanremo with the song *Nonno Hollywood* (*Grandpa Hollywood*), ranking in tenth place. The following Sanremo, his song *Baciami adesso* (*Kiss Me Now*) was a hit.

- **PFM (Premiata Forneria Marconi):** prog rock band active since 1971. Between 1974 and 1976 they entered the US charts and had an intensive live activity in the United States. Some members (the drummer, front-man Franz di Cioccio and the violinist Mauro Pagani) teaming up with two comedians and three journalists, took part in Sanremo 1988 edition with the comic project *Figli di Bubba*.

- **Prozac +:** Punk group with two women in the line-up (Eva Poles and Elisabetta Imelio). Their hit was *Acida*.

- **Virginia Raggi:** former mayor of Rome.

• **Belen Rodriguez:** Argentine-Italian showgirl, she co-hosted the Sanremo Festival in 2011. There has been a (fake) rumor about an alleged flirting with Damiano David, just because the front-man has never denied that he admires her.

• **Ron (Rosalino Cellammare):** Singer-songwriter born near Garlasco, where he will later set up his studio. He has been active since 1970 and won the Sanremo Festival in 1996.

• **Vasco Rossi:** singer-songwriter known for his rock sound and attitude. He is very famous and successful, among his hits are *Vita Spericolata* (*Reckless life*) and the generational anthem *Siamo solo noi* (*It's just us*). He led the typical life of sex, drugs, and rock and roll, because of drugs he was also arrested in 1983.

• **Daniele Silvestri:** active singer-songwriter since 1994. He alternated committed songs like *L'uomo col megafono* (*The Man with the Megaphone*) or *Il mio nemico* (*My Enemy*) with danceable songs like *Salirò* (*I will go up*). He is also important to the hip hop scene because of his way of singing, which is almost a flow.

• **Luigi Tenco:** singer-songwriter from Genoa, he started as a jazz saxophonist to become one of the most important Italian songwriters. He died, allegedly a suicide, during the Festival of Sanremo in 1967. He was in the contest with his song *Ciao amore ciao*. His death, however, has never been thoroughly investigated and it remains one of Italy's cold cases.

• **Luca Tommassini:** important Italian choreographer.

- **Francesco Totti:** important soccer player, captain of the Roma soccer team from 1998 to 2017. He's retired now, becoming a likable and ironical TV personality.

- **Mara Venier:** actress and TV host. She hosted *Domenica in* for many seasons, the "variety show" of Sunday afternoons. Therefore, the press dubbed her "The Sunday lady".

- **Verdena:** an alternative rock group active since 1995, with a woman bassist (Roberta Sammarelli).

- **Carlo Verdone:** he started as a comedian in the seventies to become one of the most popular film authors of Italy.

Websites – YouTube

Riccardo De Stefano; *Måneskin; la vera storia del loro esordio*; Youtube; November 24, 2021; available at https://www.youtube.com/watch?v=7x-n8cJXwaY.

Blick; *"Never I ever" mit ESC-Gewinner Måneskin*; Youtube; July 19, 2021; available at https://www.youtube.com/watch?v=7Jgo6Akf1e0

Endi Hamiti; *Måneskin Fun Interview*; Youtube; July 6, 2010; available at https://www.youtube.com/watch?v=WN1inOuOe_8

Måneskin Collection; Måneskin interview for HITS1 L.A.; Youtube; November 6, 2021; available at https://www.youtube.com/watch?v=lDAJWDCvxnw

Måneskin Collection; *Maneskin interview/intervista for NME: FIRSTS (Part 1)*; Youtube; October 28, 2021; available at https://www.youtube.com/watch?v=dm0hPLh9Zh0

ESCovers; *Interview #shorts – Italy #1 – Maneskin – 'Busking' – Eurovision Song Contest 2021*; Youtube; June 25, 2021; available at https://www.youtube.com/watch?v=iWWeV9u1GFA

Lafabi As; *Måneskin – Early/ Street Performances 2015-2017*; Youtube; July 14, 2018; available at https://www.youtube.com/watch?v=E_SOMB_YEfE

Musica e Tv 2.0; *MÅNESKIN raccontano da Rotterdam il loro Eurovision Song Contest*; Youtube; May 21, 2021; available at https://www.youtube.com/watch?v=jWL9cjJHmc0

Alessandro De Angelis; *Victoria 8 Yrs – SMOKE ON THE WATER*; Youtube; December 30, 2008; available at https://www.youtube.com/watch?v=FDMF-NB90JY

Ethan Torchio; *Demo 1*; Youtube; May 8, 2015; available at
https://www.youtube.com/watch?v=6YtoAKWuhHY

Good Evening Europe; *ESC 2021: Interview Måneskin –
"We are excited about being favourites to win Eurovision;"*
Youtube; May 18, 2021; available at
https://www.youtube.com/watch?v=HgfFfL6AkvE

The Upcoming; *Måneskin interview: playing in London,
new album, Simon Cowell, Harry Styles and British crowds*;
Youtube; November 29, 2019; available at
https://www.youtube.com/watch?v=O6uegqz0_Rw

Zach Sang Show; *Måneskin Talks Begging, Writing in
English vs Italian, Eurovision, Rock N'Roll & More*;
Youtube; December 4, 2021; available at
https://www.youtube.com/watch?v=o8X-iDIS6TA&t=473s

X Factor Italia; *La prima audizione dei Måneskin a X Factor
Italia*; Youtube; September 14, 2017; available at
https://www.youtube.com/watch?v=Z-YTVvUNkNE

Nofunzine Magazine; *Cesare Basile intervista Manuel
Agnelli*; Youtube; April 23, 2018; available at
https://www.youtube.com/watch?v=zP_fJ9e1M3Q&t=29s

Rockol; *X Factor 2021, Manuel Agnelli: "Paragonare i
Måneskin ai Sonic Youth vuole dire non capire un cazzo;"*
Youtube; October 27, 2021; available at
https://www.youtube.com/watch?v=lpJydrprxJQ&t=235s

Rolling Stone Italia; *Manuel Agnelli: "La ragione per cui ho
fatto X Factor è il potere;"* Youtube; September 27, 2017;
available at https://www.youtube.com/watch?v=f8UN9-qjvPo

X Factor Italia; *X Factor Replay – Live Show 2*; Youtube;
November 3, 2017; available at
https://www.youtube.com/watch?v=VyKZPnlv-8o

X Factor Italia; *I Måneskin cantano "Beggin'" ai Live di X
Factor Italia*; May 24, 2021; available at
https://www.youtube.com/watch?v=0xi9YeokShs

X Factor Italia; *X Factor Replay – Live Show 1*; Youtube;
October 27, 2017; available at
https://www.youtube.com/watch?v=ZogHI3oRCpE

X Factor Italia; *X Factor Replay – Live Show 3;* Youtube; November 10, 2017; available at https://www.youtube.com/watch?v=_bLCJ9KLfMg

X Factor Italia; *I messaggi dei Måneskin per Lorenzo Bonamano – Videodiario 2*; Youtube; November 1, 2017; available at https://www.youtube.com/watch?v=4pOvOYEEbHI

X Factor Italia; *Le imitazioni dei Måneskin – Videodiario 3*; Youtube; November 8, 2017; available at https://youtu.be/UsmBjF7HkFQ

X Factor Italia; *La vendetta dei Måneskin su Gabriele Esposito – Videodiario 4*; Youtube; November 15, 2017; available at https://youtu.be/0_Fsv-GeIFg

X Factor Italia; *i Måneskin sono pronti ad usare di nuovo il coattizer*; Youtube; November 29, 2017; available at https://youtu.be/xkPLrLehxgQ

X Factor Italia; *X Factor Replay – Live Show 5;* November 24, 2017; available at https://www.youtube.com/watch?v=Ot8gMIeHO1w

X Factor Italia; *X Factor Replay – Live Show 4;* November 24, 2017; available at https://www.youtube.com/watch?v=QHTuG_ZW7Iw

X Factor Italia; *Lorenzo Bonamano movimenta il loft di X Factor*; Youtube; November 25, 2017; available at https://www.youtube.com/watch?v=lSVVyS3BaHc

X Factor Italia; Camille & Camilla nel Loft – Videodiario 3; Youtube; November 8, 2017; available at https://www.youtube.com/watch?v=8gmVaZiuS1o

X Factor Italia; Gabriele Esposito e il dream team delle supercazzole; Youtube; November 8, 2017; available at https://www.youtube.com/watch?v=ZmSl-BggXnw

Gigi Gx; *Måneskin di X Factor: "Per Rita siamo arroganti? Noi siamo umili;"* Youtube; December 15, 2017; available at https://www.youtube.com/watch?v=a4iNhK-5Qkw

Ihatedayslikethis; *Måneskin cover Somebody told me – the Killers Acustica xf11*; Youtube; November 15, 2017; available at https://www.youtube.com/watch?v=ifTldvnbSh0

Rumors.it; *I Måneskin e i loro eccessi. Tutta la verità. Intervista dopo la finale di X Factor*; Youtube; December 16, 2017; available at https://www.youtube.com/watch?v=RC4KGpIxTH8

Tv Sorrisi e Canzoni; *i Måneskin – intervista a Sorrisi*; Youtube; January 22, 2018; available at https://www.youtube.com/watch?v=oXRS-IabP_A

Rai; *Che tempo che fa 07/01/2018*; Youtube; January 8, 2018; available at https://www.youtube.com/watch?v=cv-lclnED5g&t=177s

Rai; *i Måneskin ospiti a Radio2 Social Club con Luca Barbarossa e Andrea Perroni – Puntata del 26/11/2018*; available at https://www.youtube.com/watch?v=Ghx6PkcVJzE

Maneskin Official; *Il Ballo della Vita TOUR (Ep. 2)*; Youtube; December 22, 2018; available at https://www.youtube.com/watch?v=G1eC641TWJM

Rai; *Che tempo che fa 20/01/2019;* Youtube; January 20, 2019; available at www.youtube.com/watch?v=c9vu2ZS_ODw

Ercobbra rays; Victoria De Angelis per Freeda 2017; Youtube; November 17, 2019; available at https://www.youtube.com/watch?v=Qt64vAuNb1o

Calcutta_briciole_di; *Måneskin intervistati da Cosmopolitan*; Youtube; March 11, 2021; available at https://www.youtube.com/watch?v=uugOFykw_1U

Migliori Tik Tok – Fresh Memes; *Måneskin finale Sanremo la vittoria al festival di Sanremo alla premiazione Måneskin Zitti e Buoni*; Youtube; March 7, 2021; available at https://www.youtube.com/watch?v=Bb5YIXzbcO8

Rai; *Måneskin – Domenica In Speciale Sanremo 07/03/2021*; Youtube; March 7, 2021; available at https://www.youtube.com/watch?v=GrSpif62Xzo

Orietta Berti Fan; *Orietta Berti in "Zitti e Buoni" dei Måneskin a Name that tune*; Youtube; April 7, 2021; available at https://www.youtube.com/watch?v=p5nhYsXb1og

Radio Stonata; *Come funziona l'Eurovision Song Contest*; Youtube; March 30, 2013; available at https://www.youtube.com/watch?v=XPYwTg5mGdg

Good Evening Europe; *Press Conference: Måneskin (Italy, Second Rehearsal - #Eurovision 2021)*; Youtube; May 15, 2021; available at https://www.youtube.com/watch?v=1IIuQuO69Rg

Wiwibloggs; *Måneskin "Zitti e Buoni" (Italy) English Interview @ Eurovision 2021 second rehearsal*; Youtube; May 13, 2021; available at https://www.youtube.com/watch?v=fzoq5By-k0A

Eurovoxx; *Italy Eurovision 2021: Måneskin – Zitti e Buoni (Interview) // Eurovision winner*; Youtube; May 13, 2021; available at https://www.youtube.com/watch?v=Kzsg9Ei--pE

Il Fatto Quotidiano; *Måneskin, all'Eurovision Ziti e Buoni" senza parolacce. L'album "Teatro d'Ira". L'Intervista di FQ*, Youtube; March 18, 2021; available at https://www.youtube.com/watch?v=Kiy8nEsUxB0

Super.Winner; *I francesi non sanno perdere*; Youtube; May 23, 2021; available at https://www.youtube.com/watch?v=DLLXJPWRY4M

Calcutta_briciole_di; *Måneskin Instagram Live con Sorrisi TV 28/05/2021*; Youtube; June 14, 2021; available at https://www.youtube.com/watch?v=ytPd2oMmpuA

NME; *Måneskin on competing with Abba and Eurovision advice – Brit Awards*; Youtube; February 8, 2022; available at https://www.youtube.com/watch?v=C4yKSgC9th4

Euro Uno; *Måneskin Eurovision Livestream*; Youtube; May 27, 2021; available at https://www.youtube.com/watch?v=0TIfJJsqrW0

Anthony Rol; *Måneskin – Victoria ride fino alle lacrime e interrompono l'intervista*; Youtube; May 23, 2021; available at https://www.youtube.com/watch?v=Cexx9sis4so

Video's Stars; *Måneskin – Interview at Quotidien (subtitled in English)*; Youtube; June 26, 2021; available at https://www.youtube.com/watch?v=aLu5RAnD_0g

LeHuffPost; *Måneskin réagit à des groups de rock français (Indocine, Johnny Hallyday, Téléphone...)*; Youtube; June 25, 2021; available at https://www.youtube.com/watch?v=mqW4oPkbRvg

LeHuffPost; *Måneskin ne regrette pas l'Eurovision 2021 malgré les polémiques*; Youtube; June 25, 2021; available at https://www.youtube.com/watch?v=jwQ94Ujetcg

Madmoizelle; *Première fois – Måneskin*; Youtube; July 19, 2021; available at https://www.youtube.com/watch?v=2cnubl9f9zQ

Eurocomunicazione; *Lupa capitolina consegnata ai Måneskin*; Youtube; July 27, 2021; available at https://www.youtube.com/watch?v=0NOIbRarrto

Måneskin Collection; *Måneskin interview for HITS1 L.A.*; Youtube; November 6, 2021; available at https://www.youtube.com/watch?v=lDAJWDCvxnw&t=6s

Z100 New York; *Måneskin Describe Winning Eurovision, What Fans Can Expect from Their Tour + Workin With Gucci*; Youtube; November 1, 2021; https://www.youtube.com/watch?v=0QjsdapPUsQ

Rai; *Valerio intervista i Måneskin – Una pezza di Lundini 20/04/2021*; Youtube; April 21, 2021; available at https://www.youtube.com/watch?v=9S-y_zyoDUg

The Voice; *Special Guest Maneskin Performs a medley of "Beggin'" and "Mammamia" – NBM's The Voice Top 2021*; Youtube; November 30, available at https://www.youtube.com/watch?v=yuepbA9duSk

GQ; *Måneskin reacts to their favorite outfits – Style History – GQ; Youtube*; December 1, 2021; available at https://www.youtube.com/watch?v=DHnAI5k7srI

Mårie; *Måneskin talking about craziest fan moments "People touch my @ss" interview 1Live [English]*; Youtube; August 8, 2021; available at https://www.youtube.com/watch?v=6lw7w-3TgHo

102;7KIISFM; Måneskin talks "Mammamia"+ "Beggin'", Crazy fan Encountesr & More; Youtube; December 14, 2021;

available at https://www.youtube.com/watch?v=e-u_mPa6lTs

Articles from online magazines and newspapers

F. Galassi; *Måneskin: domenica abbiamo visto un possibile futuro della musica*; MusicaBuzz; maggio 24, 2016; available at http://www.fabriziogalassi.com/2016/05/24/domenica-abbiamo-visto-un-possibile-futuro-della-musica-i-maneskin/

I. Solari; *Victoria De Angelis senza filtri per Elle: "Che rabbia, le etichette;"* Elle; May 13, 2021; available at https://www.elle.com/it/magazine/interviste/a36382293/victoria-de-angelis-foto-senza-filtri/

A. Lepone; *Damiano e il basket prima dei Måneskin*; Il Messaggero; June 2, 2021; available at https://www.ilmessaggero.it/pay/latina_pay/il_basket_prima_dei_maneskin-5996811.html

M. E. Barnabi; *Ethan dei Måneskin, il "guru indiano" della band*; Cosmopolitan Italia; February 22, 2019; available at https://www.cosmopolitan.com/it/lifestyle/musica/a26426389/intervista-ethan-maneskin/

A. Laffranchi; *Måneskin, Victoria De Angelis: "Damiano? L'avevamo cacciato perché troppo pop. Il nome della band l'ho scelto io"*; Corriere della Sera; March 18, 2021 available at https://www.corriere.it/spettacoli/21_marzo_18/victoria-de-angelis-regista-occulta-maneskin-il-nome-l-ho-scelto-io-damiano-l-avevamo-cacciato-perche-troppo-pop-2af59f2c-8740-11eb-83f9-db14ce9af997.shtml

M. E. Barnabi; *Thomas Raggi dei Måneskin: "Sono un fissato della chitarra;"* Cosmopolitan Italia; February 22, 2019; https://www.cosmopolitan.com/it/lifestyle/musica/a26426237/intervista-thomas-raggi-maneskin/

E. Porcelluzzi; *Damiano David dei Måneskin/ Le ex fidanzate, la scuola, il basket e la Roma*; Il Sussidiario.net;

Marzo 09, 2021; available at https://www.ilsussidiario.net/news/damiano-david-dei-maneskin-le-ex-fidanzate-la-scuola-il-basket-e-la-roma/2140996/

E. Ambrosio; *Måneskin/ "X Factor? Non eravamo neppure sicuri di volerci andare!";* Il Sussidiario.net; December 09, 2021; available at https://www.ilsussidiario.net/news/maneskin-x-factor-non-eravamo-neppure-sicuri-di-volerci-andare/2260742/

Liceo Virgilio di Roma; *Intervista a Victoria De Angelis, bassista della band emergente romana Måneskin, che ci parla di sé e del gruppo, in occasione dell'uscita del loro primo singolo* Chosen; La scuola fa notizia; January 18, 2017; available at https://lascuolafanotizia.it/2017/01/18/intervista-a-victoria-de-angelis-bassista-della-band-emergente-romana-maneskin-che-ci-parla-di-se-e-del-gruppo-in-occasione-delluscita-del-loro-primo-singolo-chosen/

Redazione Digital; *La foto che dimostra che Damiano, Måneskin a parte, già al liceo sarebbe stata la crush di chiunque*; Elle; March 8, 2021; available at https://www.elle.com/it/showbiz/gossip/a35761491/foto-damiano-maneskin-liceo/

A. Nicoletti; *La vita ciociara di Ethan Torchio, l'amore per Colli e gli studi con il maestro Azeglio Izzizzari*; Frosinone Today; March 10, 2021; available at https://www.frosinonetoday.it/attualita/monte-san-giovanni-ethan-torchio-maneskin-sanremo.html

E. Assante; *I Måneskin tornano a X Factor, Luca Tommassini: "Quando Damiano mi disse che voleva i tacchi a spillo;"* La Repubblica; December 6, 2021; available at https://www.repubblica.it/spettacoli/musica/2021/12/06/news/maneskin_luca_tommassini-329185392/

Tour e sold out, i Måneskin si godono il successo. E Damiano attacca: "è tempo di rock esagerato;" Il Tempo; December 24, 2017; available at https://www.iltempo.it/cultura-spettacoli/2017/12/21/news/tour-e-sold-out-i-maneskin-si-godono-il-successo-e-damiano-attacca-e-tempo-di-rock-esagerato-1041674/

A. Orecchio; *Måneskin, dal "palco" di via del Corso alla vittoria Eurovision: storia della band rock romana*; Il Messaggero; May 23, 2021; available at https://www.ilmessaggero.it/persone/maneskin_vincitori_ eurovision_storia_band_romana_ultime_notizie_23_mag gio_2021-5977997.html

P. Giordano; *"Ehi ragà; seguite voi stessi"*; Il Corriere della Sera; December 31, 2017; available at https://www.pressreader.com/italy/corriere-della-sera-la-lettura/20171231/281986082934933

G. Sibilla; *Il debutto dei Måneskin sulla lunga distanza "Il ballo della vita"*; Rockol; October 25, 2018; available at https://www.rockol.it/recensioni-musicali/album/8257/maneskin-il-ballo-della-vita

F. Fiume; *MANESKIN – IL BALLO DELLA VITA – RECENSIONE*; All Music Italia; November 3, 2018; available at https://www.allmusicitalia.it/recensioni/maneskin-il-ballo-della-vita-2.html

A. Genna; *Måneskin; il futuro siamo noi*; Vanity Fair; October 24, 2018; available at https://antoniogenna.com/2018/10/24/edicola-vanity-fair-43-2018-maneskin-il-futuro-siamo-noi/

Måneskin cantano "Holly e Benji"; DeeJay; Il Rosario della sera; November 20, 2018; available at https://www.deejay.it/programmi/il-rosario-della-sera/highlights/maneskin-cantano-holly-e-benji/

M. E. Barnabi; *Sui suoi Måneskin Damiano non ha dubbi: Sesso, droga? Preferiamo la disciplina"*; Cosmopolitan; February 22, 2019; available at https://www.cosmopolitan.com/it/lifestyle/musica/a26426 488/damiano-maneskin-intervista/#:~:text=Sui%20suoi%20Maneskin%20Damiano %20non;Preferiamo%20la%20disciplina%C2%BB&text=A

%20Damiano%20David%20(20%20anni,Lisa%20Mancini%20gli%20ha%20proposto.

C. Desandro. *Damiano dei Måneskin e la dichiarazione d'amore a Giorgia dopo Sanremo*; Amica; February 4, 2022; available at https://www.amica.it/2022/02/04/damiano-maneskin-grazie-fidanzata/

E. Assante; *Sanremo 2021; le pagelle della terza serata*; La Repubblica; March 4, 2021; available at https://www.repubblica.it/dossier/spettacoli/sanremo-2021/2021/03/04/news/sanremo_2021_le_pagelle_della_terza_serata-290357559/

G. Sibilla; *Manuel Agnelli: "I Måneskin hanno incarnato la libertà nel rock"*; Rockol; March 7, 2021; available at https://www.rockol.it/news-720681/maneskin-manuel-agnelli-lo-spirito-del-rock-a-sanremo-2021-intervista

N. Magara; *Måneskin; il volto del gruppo cacciato via: "Voleva fare..."* Il Democratico; February 05, 2022; available at https://www.ildemocratico.com/2022/02/05/maneskin-il-volto-del-gruppo-cacciato-via-voleva-fare/?fbclid=IwAR2vpRBtzFN3H_k4vs5AgT_SqlrFDO4RQFYa3UYu1tvTlKj_BkSFz8hK7zE

S. Sirtori; *I Måneskin vincono Sanremo 2021: 5 cose che non sapete del gruppo scoperto da X Factor*; Amica; March 7, 2021; available at https://www.amica.it/2021/03/07/sanremo-2021-maneskin-vinto-5-cose-sapere/

L. Frigerio; *Sanremo 2021: l'emozione dei Måneskin dopo la vittoria. 5 cose da sapere su di loro*; Silhouette donna; March 7, 2021; available at https://www.silhouettedonna.it/news/show-e-serie-tv/sanremo-2021-lemozione-dei-maneskin-dopo-la-vittoria-5-cose-da-sapere-su-di-loro-47594/

A. Graziola; *Sanremo 2022; ecco le canzoni più vendute a pochi giorni dall'uscita: boom Mahmood e Blanco*; Soundsblog; February 7, 2022; available at https://www.soundsblog.it/post/sanremo-2022-canzoni-classifica-brani-piu-venduti-streaming-chi-sono

C. Godano; *Vi dico la mia sui Måneskin e Sanremo*; Rolling Stone; March 10, 2021; available at https://www.rollingstone.it/opinioni/vi-dico-la-mia-sui-maneskin-e-sanremo/553676/

C. Todesco; *Måneskin, il meglio e il peggio di 'Teatro d'ira Vol. 1'*; Rolling Stone; March 23, 2021; available at https://www.rollingstone.it/musica/maneskin-il-meglio-e-il-peggio-di-teatro-dira-vol-1/555136/#rabbia

M. Marzi; *Zitti e buoni: i Måneskin suonano davvero. E fanno sul serio*; Rockol; March 19, 2021; available at https://www.rockol.it/recensioni-musicali/album/9720/maneskin-teatro-d-ira-vol-i

M. Larotonda; *Måneskin: recensione Teatro d'Ira Volume 1*; Rock Shock; March 30, 2021; available at https://www.rockshock.it/maneskin-recensione-teatro-dira-volume-1/

Redazione; *I Måneskin si affidano a "Dio" per salvarsi dal plagio a Sanremo: si pronuncia la Rai*; Optimagazine; March 04, 2021; available at https://www.optimagazine.com/2021/03/04/i-maneskin-si-affidano-a-dio-per-salvarsi-dal-plagio-a-sanremo-si-pronuncia-la-rai/2084972

E. Lorusso; *Il caso Måneskin diventa virale. Damiano ai francesi "Invidiosi;"* the Italian times; May 24, 2021; available at https://www.theitaliantimes.it/2021/05/24/maneskin-paris-match-accuse/

G. Consuelo; *Måneskin: la cantante francese Barbara Pravi parla della vittoria della band*; Idealia; May 24, 2021; available at https://www.idealia.it/2021/05/24/maneskin-barbara-pravi-parla/

Redazione Web; *I Måneskin, la droga e l'ironia di Vasco Rossi: "Faccio il test anch'io?"* DeeJay; May 26, 2021; available at https://www.deejay.it/articoli/i-maneskin-la-droga-e-lironia-di-vasco-rossi-faccio-il-test-anchio/

L. Filardi; *Gigliola Cinquetti/ "Eurovision? Bravi Måneskin, nel 2022 vorrei essere ospite*; il Sussidiario.net; May 25, 2021; available at https://www.ilsussidiario.net/news/gigliola-cinquetti-eurovision-bravi-maneskin-nel-2022-vorrei-essere-ospite/2174600/

F. Volponi; *Damiano quererà la rivista francese "Paris Match?" Ecco la decisione*; Donna Glamour; June 3, 2021; available at https://www.donnaglamour.it/maneskin-damiano-querela-accusa-droga/people/

D. Seclì; *Damiano David spiega perché non quererà il giornale francese che lo ha accusato di assumere droga*; Music Fanpage; June 3, 2021; available at https://music.fanpage.it/damiano-david-querelera-il-giornale-francese-che-lo-ha-accusato-di-assumere-droga-parla-il-cantante/

G. Pasqui; *Måneskin lasciano la storica manager Marta Donà, lei si sfoga "Avete deciso di proseguire senza di me, ho il cuore spezzato;"* Il Fatto Quotidiano; June 5, 2021; available at https://www.ilfattoquotidiano.it/2021/06/05/maneskin-lasciano-la-storica-manager-marta-dona-lei-si-sfoga-avete-deciso-di-proseguire-senza-di-me-ho-il-cuore-spezzato/6221297/

Redazione; *Svelato il nuovo manager dei Måneskin, chi ha preso il posto di Marta Donà*; Optimagazine; July 27, 2021; available at https://www.optimagazine.com/2021/07/27/svelato-il-nuovo-manager-dei-maneskin-chi-ha-preso-il-posto-di-marta-dona/2183308

C. Rossi Marcelli; *La propaganda del governo polacco a colpi di slogan omofobi*; Internazionale; May 4, 2021; available at https://www.internazionale.it/notizie/claudio-rossi-marcelli/2021/05/04/polonia-omofobia

Eurovision; *Måneskin: "La vittoria dà senso a tutto quello che abbiamo fatto;"* La Stampa; May 23, 2021; available at https://www.lastampa.it/spettacoli/musica/2021/05/23/vi

deo/eurovision maneskin la vittoria da senso a tutto quello che abbiamo fatto -99417/

C. Todesco; *I rocker da tastiera sono più selvaggi di Iggy Pop: a lui i Måneskin vanno bene, a loro no*; Rolling Stone; August 6, 2021; available at https://www.rollingstone.it/musica/i-rocker-da-tastiera-sono-piu-selvaggi-di-iggy-pop-a-lui-i-maneskin-vanno-bene-a-loro-no/577153/#Part7

J. Shalvoy; *Meet Måneskin: The Italian Band That Defied the Odds and Brought Rock Bach to the U.S.*; Variety; November 9, 2021; available at https://variety.com/2021/music/news/maneskin-italian-rock-band-roxy-interview-1235108380/

Redazione Digital; *I Måneskin conquistano New York e il cuore di Drew Barrymore che li definisce "la band più sexy del pianeta"* Elle; October 29, 2021; available at https://www.elle.com/it/showbiz/musica/a38102147/maneskin-new-york-drew-barrymore/

Redazione Ansa; Måneskin send NYC crowd wild in US debut; ANSA; October 28, 2021; available at https://www.ansa.it/english/news/lifestyle/arts/2021/10/28/maneskin-send-nyc-crowd-wild-in-us-debut_58878c90-78d0-4f9a-b2f4-94428258f295.html

A. Brown; *How four '70s-obsessed Italians became America's favorite new rock band*; Los Angeles Times; December 29, 2021; available at https://www.latimes.com/entertainment-arts/music/story/2021-12-29/maneskin-eurovision-beggin-italy

Alternative Press Magazine; *Måneskin on why rock music is thriving in Italy – and across the globe*; Alternative press; October 25, 2021; available at https://www.altpress.com/features/maneskin-interview-cover-story-issue-398/

Rolling Stone; *Simone Pillon se l'è presa con il look dei Måneskin agli MTV EMA, e loro hanno risposto*; Rolling Stone Italia; November 17, 2021; available at https://www.rollingstone.it/musica/news-musica/simone-pillon-se-le-presa-con-il-look-dei-maneskin-agli-mtv-ema-e-loro-hanno-risposto/597671/#Part4

Måneskin sovrani del Festival iHeartRadio ALTer EGO di Los Angeles (video); Imusicfun; January 16, 2022; available at https://www.imusicfun.it/news/maneskin-sovrani-del-festival-iheartradio-alter-ego-di-los-angeles-video/

R. Cecchi; *Damiano dei Måneskin ringrazia Giorgia Soleri per "Coraline," "Me l'hai fatta scrivere tu"* Cosmopolitan; February 3, 2022; available at https://www.cosmopolitan.com/it/star/coppie-famose/a38968433/damiano-maneskin-giorgia-coraline-sanremo-2022/

R. Cecchi; *"La vulvodinia è una malattia seria" Giorgia Soleri non è solo la fidanzata di Damiano dei Måneskin*; Cosmopolitan; May 14, 2021; available at https://www.cosmopolitan.com/it/benessere-salute/a36416937/la-vulvodinia-e-una-malattia-seria-giorgia-soleri-non-e-solo-la-fidanzata-di-damiano-dei-maneskin/

M. Monnis; *L'intervento di Giorgia Soleri alla manifestazione di* Non una di meno *su vulvodinia e endomtriosi*; Cosmopolitan; October 25, 2021; available at https://www.cosmopolitan.com/it/star/coppie-famose/a38052150/damiano-maneskin-fidanzata-giorgia-soleri-insieme-foto-non-una-di-meno/

S. Lucarelli; *Tutti guardano Damiano dei Måneskin e non le battaglie della fidanzata Giorgia Soleri*; Domani; February 09, 2022; available at https://www.editorialedomani.it/fatti/damiano-maneskin-giorgia-soleri-selvaggia-lucarelli-ugwj6rp1?fbclid=IwAR2saQeh17RqwYCxT72eeXgic9s0mu WEPypCgIf_wTqmXkrjEQwqG5wXQX4

A. Trendell; *Måneskin on working with Iggy Pop, partying with Ed Sheeran and Eurovision advice*; NME; February 9, 2022; available at https://www.nme.com/news/music/maneskin-brit-awards-2022-interview-iggy-pop-ed-sheeran-abba-eurovision-new-album-3157797

Redazione; *Chi vuole il Ddl Zan? Favorevole il 51% degli italiani, il testo piace anche ai cattolici, nonostante il Vaticano*; Open Online; July 10, 2021; available at https://www.open.online/2021/07/10/ddl-zan-sondaggio/

Redazione Spettacoli; *I Måneskin ai Brit Awards 2022: Nessun premio ma Damiano sfoggia un sex toy*; Il Corriere della Sera; February 9, 2022; available at https://www.corriere.it/spettacoli/22_febbraio_09/i-maneskin-brit-awards-2022-nessun-premio-ma-damiano-sfoggia-sex-toy-32a161c4-89c0-11ec-ab70-14f9e3dc0d34.shtml?refresh_ce

Social Network

Mammeskin; Facebook; available at https://www.facebook.com/Mammeskin

Måneskin Official; Facebook; available at https://www.facebook.com/maneskinofficial

Måneskin; Reddit; available at https://www.reddit.com/r/Maneskin/comments/qi7fct/maneskin_in_ny_bowery_ballroom_my_experience/

The Author Bio

Meltea Keller

Meltea Keller (Martina Biscarini) was born in Empoli in 1985. She translated the first Italian edition of Harpo Marx's autobiography, *Harpo Speaks* (Erga, 2017). She wrote two music biographies (*Mannarino, Cercare I colori*; Arcana, 2018 and *Rancore, Segui il coniglio bianco*; Arcana, 2020) and a guide of Siena, (*Guida ai Palazzi di Siena*; Edizioni della Sera, 2021). She actively collaborates with ReWriters Magazine on which she has a blog called *cli-fi* focused on literature and the environment. She is the current vocalist of the all-female rock band Mumble Rumble, active since the Nineties.

Printed in Great Britain
by Amazon